INVESTING BEFORE, DURING, AND AFTER RETIREMENT

The Essential Guide to Building Wealth for Your Future With Practical Strategies on How to Invest

Dedicated to family and friendship!

ABOUT THE AUTHOR

 I don't want to bore you and take the time you have to dedicate to reading, which is much more important to have a better future but I am pleased to tell you who I am. My name is Mario Di Matteo, I have a degree in Economics and Commerce from the University of Naples "La Parthenope" in Italy. I have experience in tax consultancy and I was a teacher of the training course "Transversal skills and self-employment" in 2004 at the "Giovanni Falcone Institute", teacher of the training courses "Human resources management", "Communication technique", "marketing" , "International Economics", teacher of the training course "School In Recovery of Skills for Work Reintegration" I had the honor and pleasure of being Administrative and Personnel Director, Head of Financial, Tax and General Accounting at Spot Light Advertising S.r.l. Naples where I developed a sensitivity in noting how people are focused on improving the quality of life. For several years I have been collaborating with international insurance agencies and have professional interests from advertising to the financial market, the experience in the field that has allowed me to help many people and made me an expert in personal finance, pension and social security plans With this book I want to let you know what I have learned, to help you improve your life by planning and acting in the right way and above all at the right times. Sure this reading gives you a new boost, my wish is that you can get the best of the best.

Contents

Chapter 2: Mistakes To Avoid: Are You Doing The Right Thing?

INTRODUCTION

The evolution from a busy job to a life of leisure seems like a no-brainer, but if you don't have a few basic concepts of how to coordinate your time and the activities that will bring you happiness, you might find yourself bored, stiff, and frustrated.

There's no doubt that you've been looking forward to this stage of your life where you can put the stress of a career behind you and move ahead to enjoying the fruits of your labor. This book will help you navigate the uncharted territory, from practical advice on how to get your affairs to creating your very own bucket list of all the things you've always wanted to do.

Before you decide on any type of retirement planning, you have to be aware of the retirement plans, the information you need to get on your plan, how and when you are going to receive the retirement benefits, or what you should do if you find a certain mistake or need to ask a question. You have to be aware of the responsibilities of who is managing the plan services, and what your responsibility is. You have to be aware of how specific circumstances, like a divorce or change of employment, may affect the retirement benefits. Before you even attempt to hire the services of a retirement planner, you have to be aware of the kind of retirement plan, and the benefits that your employer is offering.

As enjoyable as retirement can be, if you begin by creating a foundation of "cleaning house" and making certain your wishes will be respected by having important documents organized, then you can proceed with your adventures without worrying about technicalities. You will find practical advice on what's important and what's not, and how to decide what works best for you.

This book will guide you with the basics of planning for your retirement, what to do with your money, how to start with debt management, and how to get the most out of your retirement years.

CHAPTER 1:
RETIREMENT: DREAM OR REALITY

Everyone will grow old. People can't be forever capable of working. At some point in their lives, they must stop working for a living and enjoy the fruits of their labor. Even if a person enjoys their job very much, they are not meant to work for their entire lifetime. Thus, each individual must plan their retirement so that they can live their remaining years on this earth in style. A lot of people believe that retirement is some sort of a reward for their hard work. But there is really no guarantee that it will be a good one. In most cases, even old people must look after themselves because no one else will. Therefore, retirement must be planned and implemented.

How to Start Planning for Retirement

An individual needs to determine what retirement means to them. People need to know how many years they still have until their retirement. Then, they must take an honest appraisal of the financial aspect of their lives. They must list all their assets, investments, savings, and debts so that they can plan a realistic budget. Furthermore, they must know the kind of life they want when they retire. This plan must be specific. The amount they may need for their retirement can be huge, but they mustn't be intimidated because there are tools they can consider to raise that amount of money.

Time can either be a person's best friend or worst enemy. It is actually a paradox of some sort. People want to maximize the value

4

of their investments yet hope that inflation won't take its toll on their savings during the same period. They may want time to prepare but want to retire very soon at the same time. Goals such as these are difficult to balance. Time can work for an individual but it can also work against them. People must plan their retirement early. They must invest for the long term to balance rewards and risks.

A lot of employees may think that their boss doesn't appreciate them. They fail to realize that there are different ways to show appreciation. The employer can offer matched and/or tax-deferred contributions to their retirement fund. Actually, individuals don't realize that this type of retirement is a regimented investment wherein contributions are pre-tax money. The employer is actually paying their employees more than they thought through the 401(k) plan.

To achieve a retirement goal, a person must know how much they need and then set out ways to realize that amount through different types of investments. In general, they must pay off their debts, use tax-deferred programs, build an investment portfolio, and schedule investment maturity dates. Car and mortgage loans and other types of consumer debt must be paid. Since most investments are charged with taxes, the person must opt for tax-deferred investments. Furthermore, an investment portfolio must be created in order as an addition to the present and retirement incomes. A person can also choose the maturity dates of their investments so they must ensure that they set these dates wisely so that money will be ready when needed.

What Are You Doing to Ensure a Great Retirement?

Retirement is something that is on everyone's mind. No one wants to work for the rest of their lives, and they don't want to end up struggling during retirement just to make ends meet. Ideally, they want to be just as well off, if not better, than they were during their working years. For this to happen, each individual needs to get started with planning for their retirement as early as possible.

Waiting until your late 50s is not a good idea because this limits the number of years that you can save for. But when you are in your 20s, you are going to college and working on paying down those student loans. In your 30s you are starting a family and saving for your first home, and by 40s you are finally hitting your stride with a good job. So where in there are you supposed to start putting your money back to help with retirement?

The truth of the matter is, you should start your retirement planning as soon as possible. If you don't already have some kind of retirement plan started, whether through your work or on your own, today is the day to start. It doesn't matter if you are in your early 20s or you are getting a lot closer to retirement than you would like to admit. Getting started on a retirement plan will help you to save money and be set when you are ready to stop working.

The earlier that you can start saving for retirement, the better. First, it gives you more years to save up money. Let's say that you are limited funds and can only put $100 a month back for your retirement. Even with this little amount, you are saving something. And if you start saving this amount when you are 25 rather than waiting until you are 35, that's an extra $12,000 (not counting the compound interest), that you have been able to save for your retirement.

The second reason that you should start saving for your retirement early on is the compound interest. When you set up a retirement fund, your financial advisor is going to invest it for you. When the investments do well, you will earn interest each year on the money you place inside. The typical return is about six percent on average each year; some years will be a bit lower and some higher.

Time Is Not Your Friend Here

When you start to reach your 50s, you must understand that time is not going to be on your side. You don't have time to make mistakes with your retirement plan like you may have had when you were in your 20s and even 30s. You don't have time to fix those mistakes or even to earn as much compound interest as you did a few years ago, which can make planning for retirement a little bit harder.

What this means is that you need to get started with planning right now. Do not wait another day. You can pick a financial advisor, specifically one who has worked with those who are limited on time before retirement, from your work, through your retirement plan, or find one of your own professionals. It doesn't matter where you find the professional, just make sure you start working with them and setting up your retirement plan as quickly as possible.

Save Up More

If you are in your 50s, it is time to start putting more money into your retirement plan so that it can earn interest and you can prepare. The good news is that once you turn 50, the IRS will allow you to place more money each year into your plan. And since it is likely you will make the most income of your life during your 50s, this is a good time to max out all your retirement accounts without having to cut out other things as much.

This means that you are able to contribute more when you reach your 50s. And if your income allows for it, you need to contribute the maximum amount that you can. This allows you to catch up, and for you to even get a tax benefit from your income as well. Even if you are not able to contribute the maximum each year because you are paying down debts or have other bills, you should make it a goal to contribute as much to your retirement saving a possible.

Protect the Income You Have

When you reach your 50s, learning how to protect your earning is very important to plan for retirement. You will find that it is hard for you to save for retirement if you must deal with medical bills from an illness or accident on top of losing your wages. A good thing to do is look at the disability insurance that your employer offers or that is in your individual plan.

Make sure that you look at what is called the elimination period. This is basically how long you will have to wait before the benefit kicks in when you get sick. The longer this period is, the more you will end up paying on your own before you get the benefits. You want to have a low elimination period to ensure that you don't lose your income and have some big medical bills as well.

Add in Some More Income

If possible, you should consider bringing in another source of income. You can use this income to pay off some of the bills that you still need to deal with or to put towards your retirement savings. To some people, this means going out and finding another job, but there are other ways that you can choose to bring in a second income.

For example, you can choose to write a book on a topic you know a lot about. You can start up a blog. Teach a class about a topic you know a lot about. Take in a roommate if you have space, take surveys, or even work on a blog. Think of some of the interests and skills that you already have and then consider how you can turn this into a side income that can help you to provide for your retirement.

Track Your Spending

Now is the time when you need to be very careful about your spending. You need to know where all of your money is going so that you can get rid of any unnecessary spending as soon as possible. After tracking your spending for just a few months, you will easily be able to see where some of the waste is, and then you can make changes. Once you find the waste, you will be able to put that money towards your retirement, saving up more than you would have estimated in the past.

All of us have ways that we are spending too much money on things. You will be able to use an online app or another budgeting source to find these things and then learn how to cut them out. For example, if you eat out too often, it is time to learn how to cook at home. If you are spending too much on a mortgage payment, it is time to downsize and look for a place that doesn't cost as much. When you cut out some of these expenses, you can free up some of your money that can then go to your retirement fund and help you catch up.

Some people reach their 50s, or maybe getting later in life than they had planned, without starting on their retirement plan. While time is not going to be on your side with this, there are plenty of steps that you can take to save up for retirement and get the life that you would like. Follow these steps, buckle down and work hard, and you will be able to still get the retirement you want, no matter your age.

Things to Consider as You Approach Retirement

Why are you retiring in the first place? Besides age, of course. Many times, people think they should retire just because of the simple fact they have reached age 65. There are many other more valid reasons to retire, but you should be consciously aware of the particular reason you are deciding on retirement.

Has Your Job Become Too Physically Demanding?

Is your job too stressful? If so, are there ways to remove or combat that stress without having to retire? What are you planning to do with the loads of time you are about to receive? Having ample time to do as you wish seems fantastic, but think about the fact that retirement may last just as long as your working years. This leaves a lot of time for just leisurely doing nothing with your life. Think seriously about how you wish to spend your remaining days before you become too old to enjoy the things that you wish you had done. Write down answers that suit you. Do not live off of someone else's feelings and thoughts for retirement.

If you can, it is of good practice to try mini-retirements before you actually take the initiative to retire. Use vacation time as a trial run for retirement. If your retirement vision is all about relocation, spend your time during retirement trial runs in new locations.

It is recommended to be flexible during retirement, especially in the early stages. Rent instead of buying and move around a bit to get a taste for newness. Don't go out and buy condos, RV's or other big purchases unless you know for sure that it will suit you during your time in retirement.

Remember that if you have a spouse, retirement should be something done as a team. This doesn't mean you necessarily have to retire at the same time, but you should talk about each of your visions for retirement and what you both want out of it. You should be ready to accommodate differences because you will be together a lot more than when you both were at work. It should be seen as a time to enjoy one another thoroughly; you will both have free time to spend as you wish. Just be prepared for the adjustment and to give one another space as needed. It is best to have a gap of at least

6 months when retiring, meaning one of you retire and the other waits at least this time before retiring. This will help make the transition easier for both of you, for one will have their sea legs equipped by the time the other retires.

Saving Money: the Secret to Success?

Retirement is one of the most challenging life transitions. It is a big challenge and anyone who goes through it must be able to plan carefully to achieve a successful retirement. Keep in mind that a lot of your decisions have life-planning and financial implications; thus, it is important for you, who will retire soon, to set goals so that you can prepare the funds to meet them.

Having worked all your life, you will naturally have mixed reactions about your impending retirement. Of course, you will be looking forward to an exciting life but you are also nervous because you will be leaving your working life behind. It is even possible that you will experience incredible stress during this transition. Financial advisors suggest that people should plan their retirement at least five years in advance. However, if it is not possible, they can have a one-year time frame as long as they are decisive and focused.

You must also take stock of your overall financial situation. Although you may not be able to make every financial decision a year before your retirement, you must analyze how many assets you have and if these are enough for you to live comfortably. The best way to do this is to have a model of your present financial situation.

There are different planning tools available online that you can use. Creating a plan may take at least 2 hours but it won't be very difficult. You just need to be thorough in planning your retirement.

Make an E state Plan

A lot of people don't like estate planning, but if you are wise enough, you must have been thinking and already planning about how you will leave your assets to your beneficiaries if you die. There are different tax benefits that you will receive just by planning your estate intelligently. In fact, estate planning is great because you will be able to make better decisions since everything will work towards effectively controlling your wealth. Estate planning involves planning for the transfer of your assets to your beneficiaries after your death. The estate consists of everything that you own like cash, jewelry, houses, retirement accounts, savings accounts, clothes, cars, land, investment accounts, and the likes. Usually, estate planning includes ensuring that the assets will be transferred to your beneficiaries, your taxes will be paid, and that there will be guardians who will be assigned to minor children.

A will is a document, which includes a plan on how the property will be distributed to the beneficiaries after you die. A trust, on the other hand, is an agreement on who will manage the assets on behalf of your beneficiaries. A power of attorney is a legal document that gives power to an entity or person to conduct the person's affairs if the latter is incapable to do so.

Estate planning must be performed even before you become legally incompetent. This means that you must be of the right age and of sound mind when you plan your estate. You must also be free from emotional stress and in good health when you draft your estate plan. You will also need the services of a certified public accountant or an attorney whose expertise is in estate planning.

Know Where to Get Income During Retirement

One year before retirement, you must have a solid idea of how much you will be receiving from your annuity, pension, and social security. You must already have a solid projection of your retirement income, including money you can earn if you continue to work plus interests from your retirement savings.

Learn to Spend Wisely

Financial planning is a personal endeavor. You must be capable of accurately assessing your financial situation and ensure that you manage your existing debts. Your cost of living during retirement will usually consist of travel, food, health expenses, insurance, and taxes. If you pay off all your debts before retirement and learn how to spend wisely, you will surely have a worry-free retirement. Your financial goals must be focused on saving and planning for your retirement. Now, if you are nearing your retirement age, you have to think of ways to ensure that your retirement savings will be enough for the rest of your life. To do this, you must have a savings plan.

Assess Needs for Insurance

If you are already nearing your retirement age, there is a great possibility that you will pay higher insurance premiums. You need to know if you need disability coverage. In addition, you may have a difficult time searching for long-term care insurance coverage. As such, you have to take out an insurance policy before you retire. You may take advantage of the services of a financial advisor so you can decide wisely.

Keep Investing Money

You may live at least 20 more years when you retire. It is actually a long time. If you don't keep and monitor your investments, your nest egg will soon be zapped by inflation. At retirement, you must switch to a conservative investment portfolio so that you can earn income and protect your wealth as well. You need to build an optimized investment portfolio for your retirement. You must carefully select and manage your assets so that you will have the retirement income that you desire when you need it. It is also important for you to preserve your wealth during retirement. Aside from having a well-diversified portfolio, you must be disciplined enough in executing your investment strategy so that you will have confidence that you will enjoy your retirement years.

Let's Live the Retirement We Want!

When you retire, there is bound to be a few changes in your lifestyle. For instance, if retirement for you means quitting a 9-5 job, it means that you will have more free time to yourself and some of that time will be spent at home.

Well, staying at home more means an increase in electricity bills, gas, heating, cooling and so on. That's just one of the many ways your lifestyle can change when you retire. Therefore, you have to start asking yourself "What kind of lifestyle do I want to have?"

A Lavish Lifestyle

Your pre-retirement days might have been filled with so much work and activities that you barely had time to do anything leisurely or have time to enjoy your money. You might have decided that your retirement time would be a time when you finally get to travel the world, wear luxury clothes, join the millionaires club, and live expensively.

The Same Lifestyle

You might also have decided that you love your current lifestyle so much that you want to continue living the same way without any major or drastic changes to your lifestyle.

Minimalist Lifestyle

Minimalism is a lifestyle that involves living with very few things and having fewer possessions. It is basically a form of simple living. If you decide to embrace minimalism, for instance, you might decide to do away with your very big home for something smaller or reduce the number of cars that you own.

Debt-Free

For some people, the focus is on living a debt-free life. If that is the case with you, you want your retirement period to be a time when you are finally free from all the debts that you owe so that you can finally focus on yourself instead of repaying debts. The kind of lifestyle you want to live after retirement is very important during retirement planning because it helps you to plan your expenses to suit your lifestyle.

Living comfortably after you retire requires a lot of planning. You have to match your expenses with your income, and if you retire expecting to have the same level of expenses you used to have while in active service, you would be making a huge mistake that might cost you your happy retirement. This is especially so because you might soon run out of funds and have to live the rest of your retirement life in discomfort, especially if you are retiring for good i.e. you wouldn't be doing any type of work or business.

When Is the Best Time to Start Planning for Your Retirement?

When some people are busy wondering whether it is too early to start planning for their retirement, others are desperately wondering if it's too late for them to start. So, when exactly is the best time to start planning for retirement?

According to various financial experts, now is the best time to start, especially if you still haven't started focusing on your future financially. The truth is that it can never be too early to start retirement planning. In the same way, it is never too late to start even if your retirement years are fast approaching.

Your Early Years

As we have already seen, the earlier the better. If for example you are still in your twenties and you are in a position to start saving for your future, then by all means go ahead and begin immediately. However, many people usually start saving for the future when they are in their 30s.

Retirement plans are usually a simple way to start if you are employed. Most employers offer retirement plans to their employees where you will have to make regular and continuing contributions. Some employers even have plans where they also set aside a contribution that matches your own contribution for your retirement.

Your Middle Years

At forty, many people will have already started planning for their future. For those who still haven't, it is not too late to start. If you are among the lucky ones who started retirement planning years ago, then forty is a good time to put in even more effort.

As most people have realized by now, goals and situations do change even in the span of a few months. For example, many people have now married since their last planning; others have started families, had disabilities, or even changed employers. This is a great age to review what you have achieved so far; it is also a good time to consider adding to your contributions or to simply determine whether your plans are still appropriate or not.

If you are 50 or thereabouts, and a citizen of the US, the federal government allows you a "catch up" option on your IRA where you will be allowed to make an annual contribution that is slightly higher than normal. If you have reasons to believe that what you have contributed so is not enough at this age, you might have to consider this option. If, on the other hand, you have been thinking of early retirement, bear in mind that drawing funds from a traditional IRA before attaining the age of age 59 ½ will possibly subject you to a 10% early withdrawal penalty.

Erik and Elodie's story

Meet Elodie and Erik! Elodie and Erik are both 55 years old. They want to retire at the age of 65. With retirement only 10 years away, they have begun to think about this transition. Throughout their careers, Elodie and Erik did very well for themselves. Recently, the pair moved to Las Vegas. Of course, in Nevada, there is no state income tax. Throughout their working careers, Elodie and Erik lived in an expensive apartment. Las Vegas is quite a change of pace for them.

For the past 30 years, Erik has worked hard and will receive Social Security. Elodie worked sporadically at odd jobs, so her Social Security benefit won't be much. That's okay though, as she'll be able to take Spousal Social Security Benefits.

It seems like Elodie and Erik might be in pretty good shape as they approach retirement. But what does their financial picture currently look like? Let's examine it. After living in an apartment for their entire lives, Elodie and Erik decided to finally pay for a house. It was not a cheap purchase either! The house is worth $500,000.

- ☞ In Erik's Traditional 401(k), there is currently $300,00 saved up. Not bad!

- ☞ In Erik's Traditional IRA, there is currently $200,000.

- ☞ Additionally, Erik and Elodie have $100,000 in mutual funds in a taxable account

- ☞ On top of it all, they have no debt.

- ☞ Erik's Social Security benefits are currently expected to clock in at a rate of $36,000 per year.

- ☞ Erik and Elodie want to retire on $6,000 per month or $72,000 per year.

- ☞ In total, this brings the net worth of Elodie and Erik to $1,100,000.

Erik and Elodie have undoubtedly done well for themselves. And retirement probably seems like a breeze, right? Well, not exactly. You see, Erik and Elodie have put themselves in a very dangerous position. They are highly susceptible to taxes and tax increases, blowing up their retirement plan. And they, like all of us, have two choices, but the only one makes sense. Do they ignore the impending tax increases and take their chances that the federal government won't increase taxes too much? Or do they take action now to lock in historically low tax rates so that tax increases in the future won't blow up their retirement?

Where Erik and Elodie Went Wrong

Let's assume, using the information we listed out above, that Erik and Elodie chose to ignore the impending tax increases our country faces. What will their lives look like at 65? And what do their lives look like as a result of not locking in lower tax rates? Here are a few of the problems that Elodie and Erik will encounter because closed the blinds on the retirement tax bomb coming our way:

Let's assume that their retirement accounts grew from $500K up to $1 million. They sadly don't actually own that $1 million. Remember, since they have never paid taxes on this money, the IRS has partial ownership of this lump sum. So, the government owns 20-30% of that amount! Further, they are extremely vulnerable to tax increases. As tax rates rise in the coming years, they are slated to own even less of their retirement accounts. Even worse, they will have no option but to pay those higher taxes since they didn't plan ahead for this possibility. In other words, because of their inaction, they limited their options in retirement.

Almost all of their Social Security will be subject to taxation. Specifically, 85% of their Social Security will be taxed. This is because their income is too high in retirement, which the IRS punishes people for by taxing their Social Security. To add insult to injury, this means that they will pay taxes on Social Security twice. First, they paid payroll taxes when they were working, and now, they are paying taxes on their benefits in retirement. Ouch.

All of these unexpected (to them) tax payments mean that they need to distribute more and more money out of their investment portfolios just to pay their tax bill every April 15. Additionally, they have far too much money in taxable accounts, which increases their income and forces them to pay even more in taxes. Lastly, Erik and Elodie do not have any tax-free income streams. Which limits their options, and frankly, their odds to have a secure, stress-free retirement.

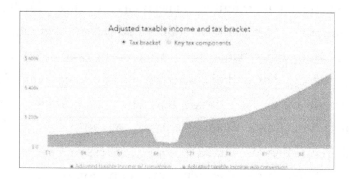

What Erik and Elodie Should Have Done

There are some smart steps that Elodie and Erik can take to avoid the tax train, though. First, they could both max out a Roth IRA. They each can put in $7,000 (since they get a $1,000 catch-up contribution), which would result in a total of $14,000 annually. Second, they could lower their traditional 401(k) contributions, and instead, put some (or all) of that money in a Roth 401(k).

One thing they'd have to be aware of is understanding that since they are making Roth contributions, they'd no longer be able to deduct these 401(k) contributions from their current income, which means they'd have to pay more in taxes this year. They would also want to make sure that they don't jump into too high of a marginal tax bracket.

Third, they can convert some of their money in Erik's Traditional IRA into a Roth IRA. The key here is that they wouldn't do this all at once! Instead, they would do it gradually, over time. Because they know that a Roth Conversion isn't about avoiding taxes (not legal, don't try it). Instead, it's about locking in lower tax rates today so that you don't have to pay higher tax rates in the future. So, they use some of the money they have in mutual funds to pay those taxes. They are also very mindful of how much they convert on an annual basis as they don't want to push themselves into a much higher marginal tax bracket.

Fourth, because they have a solid emergency fund, and are lucky enough to enjoy good health, they sign up for a high deductible health insurance plan that has an HSA associated with it. They wisely contribute $7,000 every year, and get the triple tax benefits that come with HSAs.

Putting It All Together

After taking those steps for the 10 years before their retirement, let's now take a look at them at age 65, and see how their retirement income comes together.

- ☞ Traditional 401(k): $14,000 in annual distributions.

- ☞ Social Security: $36,000 in yearly benefits.

- ☞ Roth IRA and Roth 401(k): $16,000 annual distributions.

☞ HSA: $6,000 in annual distributions (can be used to pay for Medicare and other qualified medical expenses).

☞ Total Annual Income: $72,000.

Erik and Elodie's Tax Buckets

As you could see on the chart above, Erik and Elodie wisely utilized all three tax buckets. They don't have all of their money in one bucket, which would lower their flexibility and potentially cause them to pay much more in taxes. Instead, they have practiced something we finance nerds call tax diversification. By doing such a good job with diversifying their tax buckets, it means that....

Erik and Elodie's Retirement Is Now Tax-Free!!!

How in the world is this possible!?! Let's go through their tax-free income one by one.

Social Security

Their provisional income is low enough that their Social Security benefits are not taxed. How? Because they used Roth and HSA accounts to generate income, and neither is counted as provisional income. So, since they are below the provisional income threshold, none of their Social Security benefits will be taxed. As a result, this saves them thousands of dollars per year on taxes. Over their lifetime, it will save them over a hundred thousand dollars!

Tax-Deferred Accounts

Erik and Elodie only withdraw $14,000 from their tax-deferred accounts on an annual basis, which is much lower than their standard deduction ($27,000 for a married couple over 65 as of 2016). Therefore, these withdrawals aren't taxed!

What's even better about this is that they never had to pay taxes on this money. How? Because when they were working, they deferred the taxes on it until their retirement. And now that they're in retirement since they wisely utilized the standard deduction to offset those distributions, they owe no taxes on it now. So due to careful planning, this money was never taxed!

Tax-Free

As the name states, this money is tax-free! Erik and Elodie can take money from this bucket (coming from Roth and HSA accounts) to help to meet their living expenses, along with their Social Security benefits and tax-deferred distributions. And they don't have to worry about paying any taxes on this.

Further, these distributions don't count toward provisional income, which means that we don't have to worry about Social Security benefits becoming taxable. To reiterate, here is what Erik and Elodie have accomplished:

☞ No taxes come from Tax-Free accounts.

☞ No taxes come from Social Security benefits.

☞ No taxes come from Tax-Deferred accounts.

☞ Erik and Elodie are in the zero percent tax bracket (sounds nice, right?).

Habits to Achieve the Goal

They say the intention is rather powerful, and as much as we forget to put much thought, retirement planning is inevitable. Sure, most things tend to happen by chance; how you meet your spouse and get that amazing job. You can say that life gets to act and you respectively react. The same way that things unfold in life is the same way we accumulate investment, and without some judgment and planning, soon you possess a whole collection of these investments, which are often not objective and quite often misaligned. To be able to reap maximum benefits from your investments, you need to find closure towards your investment choices. This means that you need to have a set of retirement goals before you start investing.

How Best to Set Retirement Goals

First, Determine What These Goals Are

Get clear on what you envision when you think about your retirement. Try writing a job description portfolio for your investments. At the age of 40, for example, are you likely to care about your portfolio fluctuations this week or the following month? I don't think so, and again, if you find that you still do care, odds are you lack investment understanding or you are more suited for risk-free investments; those that harbor less volatility.

If you will be good to simply stash away your savings without the possibility to withdraw until you hit your retirement age, then a 401(k) does you justice. Again, if you feel that your priorities might change with age, then a Roth IRA account better suits you. While you just never know what the future holds, it makes more justified sense to invest in both accounts and be ready for either case scenario. So, what do you do next after determining these goals?

Determine How Much You Need to Save

You can use an interactive calculation tool where upon providing your age, monthly savings, and current retirement accumulations you can automatically calculate how much you need to save monthly. Remember that the amount you determine to save monthly or yearly will depend on the retirement goals you have set, as well as the life you would want to live after retirement.

Determine Your Retirement Costs

These can be altered by a variety of factors including healthcare, everyday living, and travel needs. With these factors considered and without exempting the effects of inflation towards your savings, you realize you may indeed need much more to achieve a comfy retirement consolation.

Invest Wisely

Now that you know how much to invest, choose wisely your investment wheels in terms of bonds, stocks, and short-term reserves. Make sure the investment vehicles you choose are best suited to your preferred risk preference and the benefits. Again, if you don't have the slightest idea on how to make such decisions, consider a target-date fund. This can be a fund whose target date closely matches your retirement year.

Revisit Your Retirement Plan

Make sure to review your plan annually to make sure your investment choices and contributed amount read right. This will help you determine whether you need to transfer your investment to better profitable channels or to increase your savings.

Tips and Strategies Towards Achieving Retirement Goals

Some decisions you need to make to ensure thorough preparedness towards decades of financial freedom and security are vital, ones you cannot evade. Truth be told, as retirement age nears, it's quite certain that you tend to look back at all the events that did unfold in the course of your career, both personal and professional achievements, and also lessons learned along the way. As you look at the next approaching phase of your life with the desperate need for financial independence, you find yourself harboring more questions than available answers. You worry about how your finances will progress, will the personal savings and resources available sustain a comfortable transition? To avoid such situations, here are some tips that can help you make those vital decisions today, which could make all the difference.

Outline Your Needs, Wants, And Wishes

Determine the specific time you wish to retire and the kind of lifestyle you envision, come the retirement period. This will help lay down the expected financial needs likely to set income retirement including housing, food, transport, utilities, and medical expenses. There will also be wants, such as entertainment, vacation, travel, and social activities, as well as luxurious needs like cars and second homes.

Estimate How Long Your Personal Savings Will Last

This might not be the most ideal option here, but it is vital. This way, you can make better-informed decisions regarding the contributions towards your social security funding, pension contributions, and survivorship benefits.

Understand Your Retirement Options

Consider your options in terms of Medicare options and social security. You need to consider the best options to help leverage the benefits and suit your situation best. Again, through a financial advisor, they can help you indicate the probabilities of various options towards retirement funding.

Develop a Strategy on Generating New Income

There is nothing as compelling as when you can retire with enough security and stand the chance to keep generating new income during retirement. An income strategy makes absolute sense, especially in a scenario where you only wish to spend your income generated from interest income and dividends from investment assets. Again, a third strategy aims to generate growth and income within your investments. This helps complement other primary and most predictable income sources.

Professional Intervention

Without overlooking your probable experience in this field, planning and goal settings help you put a brave foot forward. Again, a financial advisor has in-depth expertise and harnessed skills and knowledge to help ensure thorough appropriation of every fine detail out there.

These tips will undoubtedly get you started on the retirement planning process, but an advisor can rather offer your ongoing guidance and advice. This way, you will be looking at an almost guaranteed happy retirement in the hands of an expert.

We are ready to clarify some fundamental concepts to better organize and with awareness the best strategy to adopt for retirement.

American pensions

Do you have any pensions? This does not include IRAs or 401(k)s. If you have different pension options, know what they are.

Many pensions give you different monthly income options to choose from. Each option comes with a cost. As an example, you may choose what's called a "maximum option," which means that you will get the highest payout available to you—but if you pre-decease your spouse, then your spouse gets nothing. Alternatively, you may choose another option in which your monthly payout will be less, but guarantees your spouse the same payment should you pre-decease them. Yet another option that may be available is a 50% option, where your spouse would receive 50% of whatever your monthly payout is.

These are some examples of what will likely be available to you. Generally, the more income that you secure for your spouse through your pension after you're gone, the less your monthly income will be.

If you are healthy and can afford to do so, you can "insure" your ability to take the maximum income available to you by purchasing a life insurance policy. If you should pre-decease your spouse, the pension would end, but your spouse would receive the proceeds from the life insurance policy income-tax-free. The proceeds should then be used to set up a monthly income to replace the pension lost at your death. The size of the life insurance policy would depend on the size of the pension. Should your spouse pre-decease you, you can cash in the life insurance policy for its cash value and continue receiving your highest pension payout. If you are not insurable or you cannot afford to purchase a policy, you may have to choose an option that gives you less income but insures that your spouse will continue to receive a payout from your pension.

Some people receive a pension statement every year that highlights their income options and the estimated amount they will receive. If you don't get one of these, this can be researched by going directly to the human resources department at your place of employment.

Once you have documentation on your options and corresponding payouts, assuming that you are insurable, an experienced financial advisor who specializes in retirement income planning can help you design a life insurance policy to suit your needs.

Social Security

Social security is a term used to describe a government program or system that makes use of public funds to provide economic security to the public at a certain level. The Social Security program by the United States government was started in 1935. It was formed to provide disability, old age, and survivor's insurance as well as supplementary income for the disabled and the elderly in society.

Both employers and employees in the United States are required to submit social security taxes. The money raised is then used to provide benefits to those who have attained the retirement age or are eligible based on the mandate of the program. Basically, those working today provide funds to those drawing out the benefits today, and workers today will draw benefits from workers later.

Social security benefits are based on the amount that you paid over your productive years, and how much you pay is calculated based on your income. The greater the income you have, the greater the benefits you will draw out. However, for people earning low incomes, Social Security also provides a disproportionate amount. In essence, Social Security is a program that provides for the needy in society. Every person is provided with a Social Security number. The purpose of this number is to keep track of your contributions to the program and enable you to get the benefits that you are entitled to. It is therefore important to ensure you are an active contributor to the program to enjoy the benefits.

How Social Security Works

Throughout your work life, you and your employer will be contributing to the social security system based on your wages. Presently, 6.2 percent is withheld from your paycheck and an equal amount is matched by your employer. Higher wage earners have a cap on how much of their pay is subject to social security withholdings. In 2006 that figure was $94,200. How much money you will be eligible to receive will be based on:

- ☞ How old you are when you begin to receive benefits.
- ☞ How long you were in the workforce.
- ☞ What your total accumulated earnings were.

The longer you work, the higher your social security payout will be. It is possible to begin receiving social security payments as early as age sixty-two; however, if you can wait a few more years your monthly payment will increase.

The vast majority of jobs qualify for social security. Over your working years, you need to accumulate a minimum of forty social security credits (credits are based on minimum earnings each year) to be eligible to receive benefits later. Make sure you have completed proper paperwork and your employer has your correct social security number. Your spouse or dependents can receive your benefits in monthly checks if you become disabled, or upon your death.

Benefits of Social Security

When most people hear about Social Security, they usually assume it is about a monthly check for when they retire. However, it is important to know that the benefits of Social Security are a lot more than just retirement benefits. As earlier discussed, there are benefits should one become disabled, and if you die, there are benefits to your dependents and benefits for medical care. These benefits are not dependent on your retirement because you can enjoy them if needed way before you retire. To help you understand these benefits, take a look at these facts:

In 2014, about 3.3 million children were beneficiaries of Social Security;

- ☞ 350,000 received because of a retired parent.

- ☞ 1,634,000 because of a disabled parent.

- ☞ 1,245,000 because of a deceased parent.

34% of Social Security benefits are channeled to the children and spouses of deceased, disabled, or retired workers. The average age of a disabled worker is 54 years. Statistics show that one in four twenty-year-olds today will be disabled before attaining the age of 67. These risks are real and Social Security comes in to help families that have faced the loss of income, either through death or an injury that may cause permanent disability. If you want to plan and protect for the future against possible risks, it is important to understand how the benefits work and how they apply. This information gives you adequate knowledge to enable you to decide on how you can protect your family.

Categories of Protection

There are two categories of available benefits through this program that will help you manage pre-retirement risks. These are:

☞ Worker benefits.

☞ Worker's family benefits.

These benefits are very important for your overall financial planning.

Benefits to the Worker

Apart from retirement benefits, there are two other benefits of Social Security to the worker, these are the medical cover and income cover if you become disabled. Should you become disabled, depending on your history as a worker, you can be eligible for one or two benefit programs: Supplemental Security Income (SSI) or Social Security Disability Insurance (SSDI).

The SSDI usually pays some amount of your pre-disability income based on a certain complex formula. To qualify for SSDI, it is dependent on your medical condition and work history. In essence, you must have worked for at least ten years, although many exceptions are based upon one's age.

To know how much to expect from the disability payment, you need to look into your Social Security benefits statement and see what your full benefit on your retirement age is. This is going to give you an idea of what to expect; however, you must keep in mind that various factors will affect the number of benefits to be received. Another benefit is that you may be eligible for Medicare health insurance after being disabled for 24 months.

Benefits to Your Family

In case of death or disability, certain benefits will be available to your children and spouse. A spouse is only eligible for benefits of Social Security under the following circumstances:

- ☞ If the spouse is caring for your children or child under the age of 16.

- ☞ If they have attained the age of 62 years or 60 years for survivor benefits.

- ☞ If the spouse is disabled and over the age of 50 they will receive survivor benefits.

Another factor for eligibility of these benefits for a spouse is if you were married for at least a year, while the requirements to benefit from survivor benefits is 9 months only. However, it is important to note that there are various exceptions to the requirements on the 9-month marriage length.

For children, they are likely to benefit in case of your disability or death. The children that stand to benefit are biological, legally adopted, or dependent stepchildren. Some circumstances determine the eligibility of the child receiving benefits, and these are:

☞ The child should be unmarried.

☞ Must be under the age of 18 years.

☞ Can be 18 to 19 if a full-time student in high school through grade 12.

☞ If the child is over 18 years and is disabled, with a disability that happened before the age of 22.

401(k)

A 401(k) plan is a contribution-based pension account, deducted from a person's paycheck before taxes are withheld. Many employers offer a matching benefit or a maximum percentage of a person's annual salary. As with the traditional IRA, the money is tax-deferred until withdrawn after retirement and provides the investor the benefit of being in a lower tax bracket. There is a limit to the pre-tax yearly contribution, which as of 2015 is $18,000. If you leave the employment of a company that has matched or contributed to your 401(k), there could be stipulations that will influence the account payout, so be aware of those before you terminate your position.

Since your employer is in charge of the funds you deposit into a 401k account, they (rather than you) choose how your money is invested. Many organizations offer stock in the company, bonds, other investments, or a combination of methods. Even though you don't have much control over the choice of how your money is invested, the funds are usually governed by a board of directors who must maintain a high level of transparency. If you factor in any matching benefits ($1 per $1 or perhaps up to 10 percent of your annual salary) this is a win-win situation you shouldn't overlook just because you can't pick your own investments.

Individual Retirement Account

An IRA is a savings method in which a United States taxpayer contributes a certain amount of money each year to an account designated to be drawn upon after they retire. The traditional IRA allows a person to make contributions and earn interest on a tax-deferred basis until it is withdrawn. Money put in an IRA can be deducted on a person's tax return (up to the yearly limit), which means the person's pre-retirement income will be taxed at a lower rate, and their post-retirement income and tax rate will likely be less too.

A Roth IRA is somewhat different from a Traditional IRA. You fund the account with money you've already paid taxes on and your money, including interest, will be tax-free when you withdraw it after retirement. Certain conditions must be met with IRAs and you'll want to check to make sure this is a good investment for you.

An IRA can be set up through a CPA (Certified Public Accountant) or a financial consultant. When you open the account, your advisor will help you determine if you want a traditional or Roth account and if you prefer your funds be invested in conservative, moderate, or aggressive earning methods. Don't be afraid to ask all the questions you have about the degree to which you can be involved in selecting the various funds and/or changing them periodically. Make sure you understand the financial institution's policies and fees before you commit.

Roth IRA

Consider the possibility of converting your pre-tax dollars to a Roth IRA. If it works for your particular situation, you can save tens of thousands of dollars over the life of your retirement (and beyond). You can convert your eligible assets to a Roth IRA regardless of income or marital status. You'll pay income taxes on the amount that you convert in the year that you make the conversion. As an example, if you decide to convert $100,000, that amount will go on your tax return as income for that year.

You'll need to consider whether you have enough money in a non-retirement account to pay the tax on any conversion. In addition, how much of the asset can you convert before it moves you into a higher tax bracket? You may also consider converting your pre-tax asset over years; however, each conversion amount will have its own five-year period under the five-year rule for conversions (explained below).

You are required to own a Roth IRA for five years to withdraw earnings tax-free during retirement. There are several things to consider to avoid being penalized by the five-year rule with Roth IRA withdrawals.

To withdraw your earnings from a Roth IRA tax and penalty-free, you must be over 59-½ years old; your initial contributions must also have been made to your Roth IRA five years before the date when you begin withdrawing funds. If you did not start contributing to your Roth IRA five years before your withdrawal, your earnings would not be considered a qualified distribution from your Roth IRA because of its violation of the five-year rule.

Concerning distributions, there are rules for contributions and there are rules for conversions; there are rules if you are under 59-½ or over 59-½, and there are rules for if you have met the requirements for the five-year rule and if you have not.

If you are not yet 59-½, you can withdraw contributions you made to your Roth IRA anytime, tax and penalty-free. If you haven't met the requirements of the five-year rule, earnings may be subject to taxes and penalties. If you *have* met the requirements of the five-year rule, earnings may be subject to penalties only. In certain situations, you may be able to avoid taxes and penalties.

If you are 59-½ or older, you can withdraw contributions you made to your Roth IRA anytime, tax and penalty-free. If you haven't met the requirements of the five-year rule, earnings may be subject to taxes. If you have met the requirements of the five-year rule, earnings are free from taxes. The difference here is that since you are over 59-½ you are not subject to penalties, regardless of when you take a distribution.

Roth IRA owners are never required to take distributions. This is because the tax has already been paid on the principal and the earnings are not taxable, assuming you follow the rules. Your beneficiaries, however, will be required to take distributions.

It's important to note that if you are currently required to take a minimum distribution for your regular IRA in the year you convert, you must do so before converting to a Roth IRA.

Investing Before, During, And After Retirement

CHAPTER 2:

MISTAKES TO AVOID: ARE YOU DOING THE RIGHT THING?

L ike every great thing in life, some parts need a little more attention than others. Some pitfalls can bring your entire plan down, no matter how inconsequential they may seem. The first rule of planning that we all tend to ignore is that "nothing is inconsequential." Because the truth is, when it comes to planning, nothing is inconsequential. The tiniest of things make such a great impact that you would not know what hit you when the repercussion comes calling.

In retirement planning, every step of the way is important, you need to pay attention to the tiniest of detail. Bring everything that you consider to be inconsequential to play and go through them over and over again. More importantly, you have to be careful to avoid pitfalls, as they tend to ruin everything.

Inactivity

After reading through the last pitfall, you may be thinking that the best thing to do when managing your investments is absolutely nothing. That will keep you from meddling with investments when they need time to grow.

While this is an excellent goal, having a set-it-and-forget-it mindset about your retirement investment vehicles also means you will miss out on growth. If you never review your investment strategy or regularly rebalance your portfolio, you could find yourself looking back on years of lost opportunities.

The best way to maximize your investment opportunities is to diversify your assets and meet regularly with your financial adviser to rebalance your portfolio. Joni Clark's advice is specific on this point: "Define your plan for diversifying and then rebalance regularly, whether once a quarter, once every six months, or once a year. Sell the assets with the most growth to bring your portfolio back into alignment with your plan, and use that to meet your withdrawal requirements. This approach forces you to sell high, something everyone tries to do, but few actually accomplish."

This approach is not only crucial in the lead-up to retirement, but it is also a necessary part of your post-retirement strategy. Being proactive and making savvy asset choices can ensure that your nest egg lasts for the long haul.

Taking Money from Your Retirement Plan Before Age Fifty-Nine-and-a-Half

Whether you are planning to retire in your fifties or you feel as if you need to cash out your 401(k) or IRA before hitting the minimum age requirement, you're going to have to wave goodbye to a major chunk of your money. The rules for early distributions of tax-deferred accounts are very clear: if you take your money early, then you owe Uncle Sam 10 percent of your withdrawal plus regular income taxes. The only exceptions to this are if you take a distribution for a qualified first-time home purchase or because you have become disabled. No matter how early you hope to retire, it's better to think of your retirement accounts as being completely off-limits until you hit retirement age.

Carrying Debt Into Retirement

According to the Employee Benefit Research Institute (EBRI) in Washington, D.C., as of 2008, nearly 82 percent of Americans between the ages of fifty-five and sixty-four were carrying debt. On average, these indebted 55+ households owed over $70,000.

Even though the study does not differentiate between mortgages and other types of debt, the numbers are still disturbing. Entering your retirement with debt hanging over your head means you are limiting how far your retirement income can go. And did you really save all these years just to send a big chunk of your retirement income to creditors?

While it's a good idea to pay off your debt before retirement, that is not always possible. The other option is to re-evaluate your expectations for your living standard now and in retirement so that you do not have to be in debt to maintain an unsustainable lifestyle.

If dealing with your debt is an overwhelming prospect, consider working with a credit counseling service. Please note, these are not the same as debt settlement services. Debt settlement programs will often advise clients to stop paying their bills and instead send their money to the settlement program, which will work to persuade the creditors to settle for a smaller amount. However, not all creditors are willing to accept such terms, and clients enrolled in settlement programs sometimes have to declare bankruptcy.

Taking Social Security Too Early

A too-early enrollment can cost you up to 25 percent of your benefits. Just because you can start receiving Social Security benefits at age sixty-two does not mean that you should. This is an issue that many retirees get wrong. Take the time to figure out your optimal Social Security enrollment schedule now so that you can plan your other retirement income sources around it.

Scams

Scamming retirees is a big business. According to a study on financial abuse conducted by MetLife and Virginia Tech, the elderly (defined as those over age sixty) is swindled out of $2.9 billion per year.

It's easy to see why retirees and the elderly are such tempting targets for scam artists and con men. Not only are retirees sitting on large nest eggs that they might not feel confident handling, but after years of being the head of the household and financial decision-maker for the family, they are also likely to be uncomfortable asking children or family members for advice.

Scammers will take advantage of such discomfort by being "sincere" and "trustworthy." It's an excellent idea to cultivate a sense of paranoia when it comes to anyone who seeks you out to offer a solution to a problem. It is far better for you to be the one searching for someone to help you than to accept the help of someone who sought you out.

That being said, it's also important to remember just how scammers work. Their goal is to either get hold of your money or your identity. Here are the most common ways they will try to do so:

Asking

We have gotten used to the Hollywood vision of a hacker—someone who can figure out and unlock the security systems of major corporations and government programs through their incredible computer skills. However, the majority of hackers and scammers are more like the Melissa McCarthy character in the film *Identity Thief*. In that movie, she manages to steal Jason Bateman's identity by calling him and pretending to be from his bank. He willingly gives her his Social Security number and birth date. No special hacking skills are necessary when many intelligent people don't think to question a call from an official-sounding person. Any time you get a call or e-mail asking for verification of your information, tell them you'll call back (or don't respond to the e-mail). Then, call the institution yourself to see if the contact was legitimate.

Putting Dollar Signs in Your Eyes

Believe it or not, there are still people who fall for the Nigerian e-mail scam—the one where a wealthy Nigerian needs your help transferring his riches to America and is willing to show his appreciation with a big cut of the cash. Though this is one of the crudest of the greed-based scams out there, as a near-retiree you're likely to run into many subtler schemes that promise you the moon in exchange for a small initial investment. Don't let the dollar figure of the scammers' dangle in front of you make you lose your skepticism. Things that sound too good to be true almost always are.

Peer Pressure

One easy way to make your decision seem like a no-brainer is for the scammer to make it seem as if you'll miss out if you pass up on the opportunity. If they tell you that many other savvy investors have jumped on this chance, you might find yourself following the herd mentality rather than asking the tough questions yourself.

Time Constraints

Giving you a very quick deadline for a decision is a tried-and-true sales technique that plays on our fear of losing out on a deal. You'll see it everywhere from one-click ordering on internet shopping sites to pitches stating that this particular deal on a car/appliance/real estate is only valid for one day. Scammers will often tell you that there is no time to think things over or that a price will go up if you hesitate. But there is no legitimate investment, purchase, or other deal that cannot wait at least twenty-four hours for you to sleep on it and do some independent research.

Playing the Expert

If you feel overwhelmed by financial decisions, it can be a relief to come across someone who clearly knows what they are doing, willing to make the tough decisions for you. But con artists don't actually have to know their stuff to be able to fake it convincingly.

If someone is trying to sell you on their expertise—either by assuring you that their very important position means they would never recommend something sub-par or by dazzling you with finance babble that you simply don't understand—then you need to be very cautious with their advice. Real experts know that they don't know everything, and they don't try to convince you otherwise.

For every single one of these tactics, there is one excellent solution: Ask a lot of questions. Not only will that help you to better understand exactly what is being offered (in the case that it's legitimate), but it also gives you the space to make a rational decision rather than allow your emotions to be manipulated.

Planning Late

Time passes swiftly. Some people say that time is a constant, and that who is passing is you. In your twenties, it is easy to think that you have all the time in the world and that you will have time to plan for retirement later. Interestingly, your thirties will have you singing the same song, and thinking you still have time.

You will wake up one day, and have your kids bring you a cake to celebrate your 50th birthday. At this point, it will dawn on you that you have spent over 20 of your life not saving and thinking that you had a time when in reality, you did not. Every second that passes is valuable, so when you plan late, you are not doing yourself a favor. At this point, you are probably thinking "so what if I started late? 50 means I still have like 10 years more to plan."

As the money comes in, have a sum saved up for retirement. Starting late looks like a small issue that can be ignored, it looks a lot like "when I get to the bridge I will cross it" kind of issue. But it is not. You will get swallowed by that water, and rightly so. The only way to avoid this is by starting early. Take the whole process off your mind, stop wallowing in a series of "what ifs" and start now. Because you will ask these questions again in years to come if you do not start, and it will not be a good kind of "what ifs." Regrets leave a bitter taste in the mouth.

Inconsistency

The money you need to successfully retire is much. You need to be consistent. There are absolutely no two ways about this. It is easy to say, "just this month, let us miss it for just this month." But before you know it, you are missing a few more months, and before you can say jack, an entire year has passed you by and you did not save.

The repercussion is that you will retire and then look into your account and realize that you have not saved enough. You will not realize on time that you did not save much because you will feel that other years covered up for the years you were inconsistent. They didn't, and you will find out late when you can no longer do anything about it. Inconsistency will have you looking at your accounts years from now and asking yourself what happened, where you went wrong, and where it all fell apart. Even if you are told that it was those few months you missed that became a few years, you would find that hard to believe because guess what? It was inconsequential in your opinion. At every step of the way in retirement planning, go back to the first quote we said: "nothing is inconsequential."

One Source of Income

There are two things you cannot assume. One is that you have enough time. The other is that things will always be the same. You are not in control of a lot of things; however, what you can do is make sure that you are not completely disadvantaged when the things you have no control over begin to manifest. You cannot have just one source of income when you are intentional about saving for the sake of retirement. This will breed inconsistency if, for some reason, your source of income is cut short.

For the period you are searching for another source of income, you will be inconsistent with your saving, which will, in turn, lead you to plan late. Yes, you are confident that you will not lose your job because you are so good at it. Yeah, we all thought that way before the coronavirus pandemic hit, and suddenly people were without jobs and dipping into their savings to make ends meet. In the process of dipping into savings to survive, retirement plans will take the back seat.

After all, a bird at hand... right? Not sure who came up with that analogy, but it is a lazy and silly one. Trash it. It makes you settle for less when you could aim for more. However, this is not a motivational speech, this is telling you categorically that having one source of income with retirement planning is a pitfall. It is an unwise decision to have one source of income on a normal day, it is worse when you are saving for something as important as retirement.

Coming up with a 401k or more requires consistency, the kind you cannot compromise on. This means that whether there is a pandemic or not, you are saving, whether there is an issue with the markets or not, you are saving. Diversify your streams of income immediately. Find other things that could get you money, invest too, do anything that could legitimately fetch you more money.

Ignoring Market Inflations

There is no tangible reason why anyone should not pay attention to the inflation and the deflation of things when they are saving. Know that something that costs $1 could cost $10 in a few years. Before you shrug and say "it is normal' know that, the reason the inflation that is currently happening doesn't affect you so much is that your salary is inflating too. Try shrugging when you have no source of income but your retirement plan, which is not doubling as it stays in your account. Is it still a struggle though?

No, because it has suddenly dawned on you that goods will increase, services will increase, and your money will not increase. Sooner or later, the money you have would be enough to buy you what you need. However, this is a way to avoid this pitfall, and that is by investing in real estate. When the prices of goods and services go up, real estate does too, which means you can make money from it.

As the value grows, you can sell the property and make enough for you to get the things you need, want, and more. Never ignore how high the market can inflate goods. Every year, it seems like an extra dollar or more is added. Ignoring this is setting you up for a pitfall.

Ignoring the Place of Professional Help

We may have underrated the importance of Google and what it offers, but we underestimate the importance of talking one on one with a professional. Yes, you seem to have all the basic knowledge, but you may not see something unless it is shown to you by someone else. For something as huge and long-term as retirement planning, you need a financial advisor. You need someone to walk the entire road, or better yet, set the lights that would guide your paths. Walking this route alone is usually a bad idea.

This book is one of the companions you need, but you still need a person who is a professional to walk the road with you. Ignoring the place of professional help is a pitfall that no one prays to be caught in. They understand things and are willing to teach you the things that they understand, just to broaden your knowledge.

If you let them, they can go through your earnings and then help you create a retirement plan that would work perfectly for you. They will act as advisors, strict coaches, and the ones who constantly remind you that you are on a mission to not end up old and broke. You need a financial planner.

Moving Jobs

In some companies, they unlock the employee packages that include retirement benefits after a year. However, if you keep moving jobs, you may never get to settle down to the point where you are collecting small dividends for retirement savings. If your employer works with stock options, in some places, you do not have full ownership of that stock until you have worked in a company for at least five years. If you have worked to that point where you now have full ownership of those stocks, it does not make sense to jump from one job to the other when you are saving for retirement. It will breed inconsistency, and by now we have already agreed that inconsistency is not something that should be allowed when it comes to retirement planning.

You may think that this is not that big a deal, and in all sincerity, it isn't. However, if you are serious about retirement planning, moving from one job to the other and depriving yourself of the chance to get to the point where you are now fully enjoying these employee benefits is unwise. If a job pays well, you are at the benefits stage, stay put and save up for your retirement plan.

Jumping Into Investments

Yes, investments will help you make sure you have a steady stream of income even when you no longer work. However, a bad investment will have you wishing you did not bother in the first place. A financial planner will help you go through investment options, then go ahead to help you make the decisions on the one you want. Jumping into investments without the proper help that is needed is setting yourself up for failure.

Retirement plans are beautiful until you are drowning under the waters of a bridge you said you would cross when you get there. Plan, strategize, save, and more importantly avoid mistakes

CHAPTER 3:
PLAN FOR HEALTH CARE EXPENSES

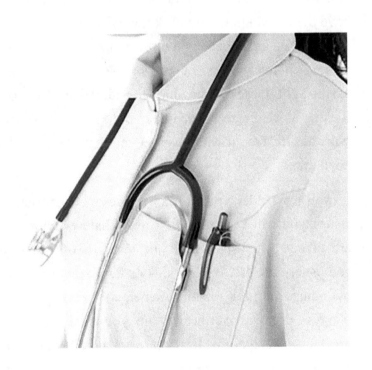

D ear prospective retiree, this is probably not news to you, but you are getting old. Was that harsh? Maybe. But you need to realize that you are not going to be as sharp and healthy forever; you will need healthcare. Keep this in mind, the cost of healthcare is constantly increasing, and by the time you are older, it would have increased a lot. Do you know what this means? You are not earning, you are dependent on the money you saved, which means a large chunk will be cut out for the sake of healthcare. When saving, put these things into consideration. You probably are looking at Medicare for people over 65, now aren't you? Wait till you are sick, then it will dawn on you that Medicare doesn't cover anything.

As you grow older, your bones will age and your organs might have issues, you will need medical care. Whatever retirement plan you are taking, it must account for the cost of healthcare or it is completely useless. If your kids or family members have to shell out a huge sum for a medical emergency because your retirement planning did not cover health care, you are doing them, and you a great injustice. Ignoring healthcare is a pitfall you must not fall into. You will be too old to regret it when it happens, too old.

Respect Your Health

One of the most important things you can do as you go through the retirement journey is, to be honest with yourself. Be honest about your saving and spending habits and your ability to change any of those habits if you need to along the way.

At the very top of the honesty, the list should be your health. Be honest about how you take care of yourself and your ability to care for yourself later in life. If you don't make your health a priority, your retirement may become a much more complicated and difficult period for you and those around you.

Of course, health concerns may arise that are out of your control. Even if this is the case, you can also maintain a healthy lifestyle to prolong your life and make it as comfortable as possible in your retirement years.

According to a Merrill Lynch report titled *Health and Retirement: Planning for the Great Unknown,* healthcare challenges pose a double threat to your retirement. First, expenses can be high, unpredictable, and deplete your retirement savings quickly. Second, if you are forced to retire early because of health issues, you will lose earning years and savings potential.

Estimate of Out-of-Pocket Health Care Costs

The chart below shows an estimate of out-of-pocket healthcare costs based on one's estimated length of retirement in years.

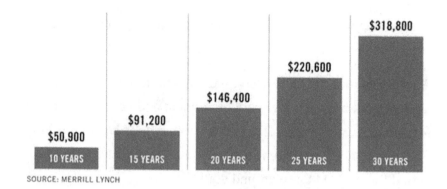

SOURCE: MERRILL LYNCH

The report points out an AARP (American Association of Retired Persons) survey that found two-thirds of large companies offered health benefits to retirees 25 years ago. Today, only one-third of large companies offer retirement health benefits.

As shown in the chart above, the longer you live past age 65, the greater the out-of-pocket expenses you will pay for healthcare. It's a difficult position to be in, even if you have done everything "right" in your savings and retirement budgeting.

The Role of Health Complications

Let's start with the good news. According to the Merrill Lynch Report, retirees say health is the number one factor in happy retirement. Also, as the baby boomer generation ages and retires, many of them are taking a much more active involvement in their own health and the healthcare system on which they will depend.

Compared to their parent's generation, baby boomers are:

☞ More than four times more likely to say they actively research health information (79 percent versus 18 percent)

☞ Two and a half times more likely to say they are proactive about their health (75 percent versus 30 percent)

☞ More than twice as likely to say they question doctors' orders (70 percent versus 29 percent)

☞ Twice as likely to say they view their doctor as an ally or partner who works with them to optimize their health (46 percent versus 23 percent)

Generational thinking is shifting to some degree, and Americans are changing the way they think about health as they age and begin to need healthcare. The bad news begins when health complications occur. The US Department of Health and Human Services says that nearly 40 percent of people over the age of 65 years will spend time in a nursing home. Thirty percent will stay less than three months, but 50 percent stay more than a year and 20 percent stay longer than five years.

Long-Term Care

One thing to think about is how best to incorporate long-term care into your retirement budgeting process. As you know, Medicare is not free, and it does not cover all your needs. Plus, average nursing home stays are more than two years, so you have to consider adding a budget of an extra $200,000 (not including inflation) into your savings. Working with your financial planner and/or accountant may help. Even if you don't need a nursing home, extra help and home healthcare costs add up, with some estimates at $40,000 per year. This is the self-insuring process where you save what you need. What else can you do? If you decide to get long-term care insurance and pay premiums in exchange for healthcare services, you will need to consider a few things:

When planning for long-term healthcare, consider the timing of your decision. Insurance premiums are lower the younger you start (e.g., 55 rather than 70). Your health will be better when you are younger and not affect your ability to getting long-term health insurance policies. Also, if you are still working when you take out the policy, that income can help you pay for premiums into retirement.

Thinking about it sooner rather than later will help you better prepare for the worst while hoping for the best. The plan will have already been made and incorporated into your budget, and you will be acting rather than reacting when it is too late.

The Merrill Lynch study discusses the following steps to prepare for retirement healthcare expenses both for pre-retirees and retirees:

- ☞ Maintain a healthy lifestyle and wellness regimen. Even if you start later in life, the improvements you make can help you maintain good health in your retirement years.

- ☞ Take proactive steps to stay financially prepared for healthcare expenses.

- ☞ Estimate and begin saving for out-of-pocket healthcare expenses.

- ☞ Learn as much as you can about Medicare and what it can and can't do for you

☞ Make sure you plan for lost income if you fall ill unexpectedly before retirement.

☞ Talk to your family and advisor about healthcare topics and decisions.

☞ Create contingency plans for healthcare problems and expenses for yourself and your spouse.

☞ Research all long-term care options and prepare for your needs as best as you can.

Other Options

If you are under the age of 65, do not have Medicare, and are not covered through an employer, the Affordable Care Act allows enrollment through its Health Insurance Marketplace so you can buy insurance that fits your needs. Open enrollment has come and gone, but there are special enrollment periods. There is also potential for tax credits and lower out-of-pocket costs depending on your income and household size.

If you have coverage through an employer, you are considered covered under the law. If you have retiree coverage and want to buy a Marketplace plan instead, you can. However, you will want to note the following:

☞ You won't get lower costs on Marketplace coverage.

☞ If you voluntarily discontinue your retiree coverage, you won't qualify for a special enrollment period to enroll in a new Marketplace plan.

☞ You won't be able to enroll in health coverage through the Marketplace until the next open enrollment period.

☞ If you are older than the age of 65, refer to Step 7 where Medicare, its eligibility requirements, and automatic enrollment for certain types of plans is described in detail. Other plans can be purchased for greater coverage.

Health Savings Accounts

Saving for healthcare can be a daunting task, especially given all the saving that's just associated with living expenses. If you have exhausted Medicare and your own savings options, other alternatives can help you pay for medical expenses.

Health savings accounts (HSAs) are personal savings accounts that allow you to put money (sometimes pretax and sometimes posttax) into an account to pay for medical expenses. The best part is that the money contributed to the plan is not subject to federal income tax when you deposit it, as it grows, or when you withdraw it, providing you a "triple tax savings." Sometimes employers offer these plans to employees, and the money can be rolled over, when needed, to other HSAs.

An HSA can provide you with the following:

☞ Control of how much money to put away, which expenses to pay, where to hold the money, and how to invest it.

☞ The money belongs to you, and there are no "use it or lose it" rules.

☞ Your contributions are allowed as a tax deduction.

☞ Your contributions can be excluded from your gross income.

☞ You can use HSA money to pay for current or future medical expenses.

Also, once you turn 65, you can no longer contribute to your HSA. You can take money out of it tax-free. Much like 401(k)s, employer HSAs offer investment options that can involve risk and loss. It's best not to put all your HSA money into one type of investment. This is money for medical expenses, and you'll want it when you need it. Think of your stage in life, just as you would with your 401(k), and choose investments that reflect your risk tolerances and goals.

HSAs should not be confused with flexible spending accounts (FSAs), which do not allow you to roll over the money you have not used. They are accounts with finite periods to use them. You can use FSAs to pay healthcare bills, but you will lose the money if you don't use it before the year's end.

Asking the Right Questions

What kind of consumer are you? Are you asking the right questions? Are you asking them of the right people? Are you getting the information you need to be informed and educated?

These are the most important steps you must take, even with the provisions of Medicare, savings, and HSAs. It is important to identify the best, most cost-effective providers to manage your care into retirement. Fidelity Investments discusses four types of providers you should identify for the best care possible.

☞ A primary physician.

☞ A specialist for any existing conditions.

☞ An urgent care provider.

☞ A full-service hospital.

Fidelity also recommends that you are prepared to give your provider information. Ask the hard questions to get a clear description of any diagnosis and the doctor's proposed plan. Know what you are paying for—the fees, charges, and out-of-pocket costs you can expect for treatments or recommended treatments.

The bottom line is to prepare for any possibility. You may feel well today, but you don't know what is lurking down the road. Medical costs can be extremely high, so solid savings and preparation, just as with your retirement savings, will save you from added stress and debt later on. When considering your health needs, hoping for the best and preparing for the worst has never been truer.

The Recap

Almost no one wants to talk or think about long-term care, but with our aging population living longer and the increased risk of chronic diseases as we age, it's a topic we must confront.

Many people are inclined to gamble that "it won't happen to them," but statistics suggest that during your retirement, you or your spouse are very likely to need some kind of long-term care. It's a good idea to review the statistics and be familiar with the probabilities.

Cost is the main reason most people don't obtain long-term care coverage, but it is far more costly to pay for long-term care out of pocket than with a long-term care insurance policy.

For some reason, many people worry thinking "What if I never use it?" regarding long-term care. Yet most people are glad they have homeowner's insurance in case the house burns down, even though for most people that will never happen. Having protection in the event of a long-term care situation offers the same peace of mind: your entire nest egg won't be decimated to pay for care at the end of your life.

CHAPTER 4:
THE RIGHT AND WRONG NUMBERS
IN THE WORLD

There's a lot that you don't know about the next couple of years. There's even more that we don't know about the future as it continues. This includes tax rates, inflation rates, what your health care will cost, the returns you will get from your investments, and much more.

There are a lot of factors that you have to try and you'll have to make some assumptions as well. There is no cookie-cutter method to approach your finances. No computer algorithm will be able to provide you with a game plan of how to manage them. You'll have to start your planning with some reasonable ideas.

Your income allocation plan will go through what your finances will look like year by year. When someone looks at income allocation, they usually start with social security and guaranteed pensions that you have. These are the income sources that won't go away until you die. Some pensions will have some benefits for any survivors you have, but that's usually less than what you were getting.

Now, we have to get from all that guaranteed income to the growing income that has been requested. You'll build from those first sources. This involves a lot of creativity and sometimes fun for the person that's doing income allocation. When you're trying to plan out your income for the rest of your life, there are a lot of ways that this can go for the average person. There may be an option that is above all the rest, but more often than not there is a combination of options that gets put into effect. We're going to go over some options that might help you when it comes to planning out your retirement income. Remember that some of these will not work for you while for others may seem perfect. Everyone has different goals for their money and what they want to do.

We'll say that your monthly expenses are roughly $6,000. Between pensions, Social Security, and a couple of other guaranteed sources of income, you'll want to cover almost all of that income. You might be able to use a reverse mortgage in this too if you do it well. You might also want there to be roughly $15,000 funds every year for any travel, gifts, hobbies, and other things. We will look to other sources of income that are more probability-based to try and get the money for your more fun parts of retirement.

However, most people like knowing that their financial obligations aren't at risk because of the market. You don't want to worry or stay up at night worrying about your money. This brings up back to the three buckets of risk and the three tax buckets. Many people who want to have guaranteed income beyond what the pensions and Social Security provide will put a similar amount into the Principal Protected bucket. This means that they'll be covered when it comes to their financial obligations almost all the time. Of course, it still might not cover it all of the time. Some people have different goals.

People that had invested their money in CDs that had roughly three to six percent of interest were struggling to make ends meet and how to actually use the principal of the accounts. There was a similar problem when it came to reinvesting in bonds and finding that there were lower interest rates. While the principal is protected, if inflation is higher than the interest that you are earning after taxes, then you're not going to have as high of purchasing power as you started with. This means that while your bank account doesn't look it's decreasing in value; you are losing some ability to purchase the same stuff that you are now. CDs also don't have much protection when it comes to risks associated with longevity. Annuities can have these protections that might make them a better option.

Saving for Retirement

A good many of those folks tell me they have doubts. Some have small doubts and others know they are in trouble. And of course, some people have no idea and don't even know how to go about answering that question. Has anyone ever asked you?

By the way, for those who believe they are in trouble of outliving their retirement savings and then completely relying on Social Security, there is a pretty common reason they want to explain to me. What do you think is the biggest reason that people who have doubts is? It was because of too much debt over their working lifetime. I'm not judging, but this just makes common sense, doesn't it?

Over my many years of being a professional financial planner, I have found that one of the biggest reasons why many folks have not saved enough for retirement is that they carried too much debt— especially "bad" debts. Too much debt equals big monthly debt payments, which hampers the ability to save for retirement.

What do I mean when I say "bad" debt? I mean virtually all types of non-mortgage debt, credit card debt, consumer debt, personal lines of credit, student debt, etc. Not that having a mortgage debt and monthly payment that is oversized concerning your income is good, but at least you get a tax deduction, and usually that debt has a relatively low-interest rate too.

Do these comments make sense to you? Is bad debt the biggest reason that you or someone that you care about hasn't been able to save enough to retire the way you/they dream of? Unfortunately, for 10,000's of business owners, that will not likely be the case. All too often, they are the business, and when the owner leaves, there's not much left to sell. Certainly not for anywhere near what they might be planning on. Of course, there are many exceptions where a business has been built to the point where it does not depend on the owner being there every day, and the business can be sold for a substantial sum of money.

If you own a business, it may be a very smart idea to speak with a professional business broker who could give you some guidance of how "sellable" your business is now and what you will need to do to increase its value to a potential buyer.

The next section is written for those who are still saving for retirement (or perhaps to teach your adult children).

Putting an Income Plan Together

Let me ask you a question. On any new thing that you have ever tried to learn, were you great at it right away? For example, would you have called yourself a proficient golfer the first year or two of learning the game? Or how about cooking? Home repair? Becoming a parent? There was no owner's manual on that one. I know I made a ton of mistakes and had a deep learning curve on this one! Think about anything new that you tried to learn in your past… and how long or difficult it was for you to master it. Just like most things in life, there is a learning curve on any new skill. Only a small percentage of us are immediately proficient in any new area.

Most folks only retire one time. They've got one chance to make it as good as they can. Sometimes, mistakes can be fixed without too much damage, but other times, that's not the case. Although no book or adult education class can truly prepare most people to plan the next 30+ years of their life, what you will read on these pages will at least help you be aware of some important things that you might not know about.

At least financial advisors that specialize in retirement income and distribution planning (vs. accumulation) have done this before. In addition to specialized training, they probably have years of practice (on other folk's retirements!). So certainly there has got to be some benefit and added advantage of using a professional for such an important endeavor as planning for a 30+ year growing income stream using all of your available resources (Social Security, pensions, savings, home equity, etc.)—especially if you don't feel (and probably rightly so) 100% capable. This is where a retirement income Sherpa can make all of the difference.

You might remember the "what's your number" commercials on TV. You know, the ones that had people carrying around big orange numbers that represented the amount they would need to retire. Their retirement savings goal. What number did you think was "your number"? Did you have any idea where to start making your number goal? Is it $350,000? $1,000,000? $2,500,000? Well, maybe you saw an article in *Money Magazine* years ago that talked about the "4% rule". Here's what it is (or was) all about.

Retirement Income Planning

There cannot be a cookie-cutter approach or perfect formula that you put some data in the "black box" and out pops a computerized income model that says where to invest, which investments to tap, and when to optimize a long and prosperous income plan with as much predictability as possible.

When I do a retirement "income allocation" plan for a client, one that shows them how and where we are going to, year by year, fulfill their requested growing income—inflation until age 100 (longevity)—I start with Social Security and/or guaranteed pensions on the left side of the spreadsheet.

Those guaranteed income streams that last until the person passes away—sometimes pensions have a survivor benefit, but not usually 100% of the income—form the basic building block of the retirement income plan. Then, in very simple terms, we just need to fill in the gap of that guaranteed income and the requested amount of growing income. We need to build the spreadsheet left to right.

This is where my job becomes both creative and fun, as except for the wealthy, there are many different directions someone could go to solve the lifetime income problem. Sometimes, one solution is clearly superior to others, but I often use a combination of solutions best meet the plan.

In the pages that follow, I'll give you a few solutions that may provide you with the insight to plan your own retirement income. As I'm sure you can appreciate, no single solution for income is right for everyone. People have different income and legacy goals, life expectancies, risk tolerances, and several other personal circumstances. Begin with the end in mind.

The amount of retirement savings, real estate, life insurance, pensions, potential inheritances, and the like, all must play a critical role in determining the best course of action. And of course, since the future is totally unpredictable, we must add that into the mix as well. So, this is where the "safety-first" part of your total "income allocation" comes into play.

In essence, we want a large part of our "non-Social Security and pension income" to be guaranteed. At least enough to cover most, if not all of our basic retirement living expenses. If we have basic monthly retirement income expenses of $6,000, we want Social Security, pensions, and some other guaranteed sources of income to provide most, if not all of that income. Perhaps a wise use of a reverse mortgage too.

But if possible, most folks would rather "know" that their "monthly nut" (financial obligations) as one client of mine calls it is covered for as long as they live, with no market risk and no worries, no sleepless nights. Just peace of mind. In other words, the amount of extra monthly income, above and beyond Social Security and any pensions, to handle most or all of their ongoing financial obligations can often be funded by the amount of their retirement savings they told me that they wanted in their Principal Protected bucket. Not always, certainly. Everyone's situation, needs, and goals are different.

So, what investments and/or products do I typically use for this "bucket" as part of the income allocation plan? Well long ago, I had a number of my clients kept one or two years of this non-Social Security/pension income extra income in the bank: CDs and savings accounts. If the market was down, rather than selling stocks/mutual funds at low prices (sequence of return risk), we'd fund our income needs from the cash account.

Having some cash on hand allowed our stocks to recover from a downswing—without selling stocks at low prices (and not having those shares available to eventually recover). When the market recovers and raises, some of those gains are taken to replace the bank savings for the next potential market downturn. But with these FDIC investments, paying nearly no interest over the last 5 to 6 years, for most of my clients this is not a great option for this strategy. And as you know, CDs do not offer any lifetime income guarantees.

Although the principal is guaranteed with CDs, real inflation (the kind that you and I actually see in "real life", not what the government tells us it is) is running way higher than what the bank pays us in interest. To add insult to injury that interest is usually taxable, whether we spend it or not. Paying taxes on puny CD interest income is a slap in the face to folks on a fixed income. But it's the law.

Many people do not realize this, but there is a sequence of "interest rate" risks with CDs and savings accounts. Just like the last half a dozen years, there will be a period of extremely low-interest rates again sometime in the future. I worked with one CPA who told me that many of his elderly clients who lived on "safe" CD interest-only (when rates were 3%-6% in the mid-2000s) were now having to deplete principal to make ends meet. The same thing could be said for those who are re-investing in bonds at much lower interest rates than they enjoyed before.

So yes, your principal is safe with these bank FDIC savings vehicles, but when inflation outpaces your after-tax earned interest, your purchasing power decreases. Your bank account statement does not show a decrease in value, but when you go to spend those assets when inflation is higher than your net after-tax interest earned, you have a loss of buying power. You need more dollars to buy the same amount of "stuff."

And of course, CDs do not give you any protection from longevity risk either. But many annuities do include fixed indexed annuities with an income rider. Let's look at what many of my clients decide to use for most of their "Protected Principal" risk bucket and exactly why they often choose it.

78

The Challenges of Retirement

Financial Challenges

Retirement for many people is as scary as it is exciting. You have worked your entire life to earn enough to live your remaining years peacefully and without worry. But nowadays, more challenges are arising in regards to the community of retirees. Throughout your working life, you have accumulated assets to aid you in cushioning your retirement. From participating in the 401(k) plan and maybe even establishing yourself in an IRA or other retirement plan, despite how much you have contributed, times are continuously changing, which is why it is absolutely crucial to plan out how to convert your assets into the right kind of income.

Many retirees find themselves only having Social Security and their retirement savings to get them by for the remaining years of life. Unlike previous generations, you may not be under a pension plan from where you worked, so you might be totally on your own when it comes to overcoming these challenges when stepping into retirement.

Longevity

We all have a chance to live longer or shorter than anticipated. A recent study conducted in 2015 by the Society of Actuaries showed that a fifty-five-year-old male has around 76% chance to live until the age of 90, while a female of the same age has an 82% chance of living to their 90s. What does this mean? It means that you may spend just as much time in retirement as you did working in your career. Creating enough income to cover day-to-day expenses for 30 or more years is a daunting thought and task, especially in a world where there are fewer opportunities available to those of retirement ages to earn income.

Volatility

Environmental disasters and other events are not predictable, such as earthquakes, tsunamis, 9/11. When these types of events occur, you can almost always predict an impact on the financial markets. These events are always a possibility, but should not hinder your ability to trade your assets. However, you should be wary. Trading nowadays is completed 100% electronically and at the speed of light. To get the most bang for your buck, ensure that the climate of conductive trading is at least somewhat balanced to produce greater volatility.

Inflation

Inevitably, the prices of goods and services increase annually each year. Even though the inflation rate has dropped and maintained in recent years, hovering around 1 to 3 percent can still have an impact on your purchasing power. For example, today's $1,000 may only be able to purchase $550 in goods 30 years from today with a 2 percent increase in inflation. With 3 percent, that grand $1k will only be able to buy you $400 worth of goods and/or services. And who is to say inflation won't exceed past 2 to 3 percent? That means the results could greatly impact your ability to live without stress. Retirees living on a fixed income can run into many difficulties when it comes to making ends meet later down the road. And the goods and services that tend to go up the most are those utilized by retirees themselves.

Taxation

If you were within the high tax bracket for the majority of your life, retirees must be aware of where their assets are invested. Hedge funds and mutual fund managers tend to not consider taxes when seeking out profits. The turnover of portfolios can be high and short-term capital gains, which are taxed at regular income rates and tend to be generated in abundance. Mutual funds also have the potential to create "phantom income," which means its distributions or capital gains are reinvested in additional fund shares. You never see them but are still continuously taxed on them. Many investors find themselves paying taxes of distributions of capital gains when their other fund shares have majorly decreased in value within the year.

Leaving Legacies to Your Loved Ones

While there are retirees already stressing out about how they are going to live in their elderly years, there are plenty who have no concerns when it comes to making ends meet during their retirement. However, every single retiree has the challenge of leaving a legacy to loved ones. In fact, this is typically a primary concern, especially if it is related to estate taxes. As much as a 40 percent reduction to the estate tax can occur, depending on where you live. Erosion is a profound issue.

How to Combat These Financial Challenges

Back many years ago, the go-to strategy as you retired was to reallocate your portfolio(s) from equities to fixed income and live off of the interest it generated. Today, the all-time low of interest rates and increase of life expectancies have eradicated this method.

One strategy to consider as you reach retirement age is the 4 percent solution. You can avoid the total depletion of your little nest egg by withdrawing 4 percent per year from your assets. This strategy is not foolproof by any means because it is based around the possibility of living only an additional 25 years after initial retirement. There is a great possibility you could live longer and run out of money to live off of.

Another strategy is to identify your sources of income that is guaranteed to you. Look into variable annuities that are issued by insurance companies that offer professionally managed investment options that are moldable to shape around your life. Similar to the IRA or 401(k) plans, variable annuities have assets that grow tax-deferred until they go to be withdrawn by the owner of the contract. This means that when it comes time for you to retire, you can choose to receive life contingent income distributions. Depending on the options you choose, you have a good chance of being able to receive income that is guaranteed to last as long as you live.

What to Do With All This Time?

This question is often referred to as "the retirement problem." There is a combination of excitement paired with anxiety within those that are approaching retirement age. It is exciting to have free time and not be bound by work and its deadlines, yet, anxiety takes hold when it comes time to bear the questions of what to do with all the ample time you are about to have and how to figure out how much you can and can't spend. Much of the population imagines what their retirement will be early on and create big plans of what they wish to do with all that time that is still within their budget.

Once we reach retirement age, people tend to have major doubts about what is to come next for them and their lives. Another realization for retirees is recognizing that this is the last stage of their lives. Throughout their youth, they knew deep down that life is short and flies by fast, but during those years they were busy building careers and families, which kept the emotional recognition of this inevitable fact at bay. This is enough to make anyone scared of the future and the anxiety of trying to make the best of what they have left come to light.

While time and money go hand in hand, money is the more practical of the two concerns. Many retirees become more anxious about having enough money to get by rather than how they will be spending the remainder of their time here on earth. More and more retirees are becoming less sure about what their income during retirement is going to be and where it is going to take them. Money is not all one needs to have a successful retirement. In saying this, those approaching retirement needs to have more than just a financial plan. They must also have some idea of what they plan to do with the rest of their time to be engaged in the last stage of their life while still being productive.

Take the time to self-reflect on your life and yourself as a whole. What do you enjoy about your job the most? What do you like to do the most during your hours away from work? If you have no idea, perform this mental exercise. Imagine that your office is closed for an entire week. Ask yourself what you would do with that time off. If you have no clue, think about your hobbies or activities you wish to take up and experiment with. Think about places to volunteer. Things like this. What makes your soul light up? What makes you tick? It is important to dig deep about this because you are going to have a lot of time to kick back and relax, but I assure you that just relaxing will not suit you in the long run. Are there things you have always wanted to learn? Are there ways you wish to make the world around you a better place?

Inevitably, there are going to be things you pursue in your retirement age that you are not good at or you do not like as much as you thought you would. It is important to seek out classes to better specific skills so that you are not constantly put down by not being able to accomplish what you wish to.

If you are someone that has the urge to continue working, then perhaps you should consider a phased retirement, which means you can work part-time to still earn a paycheck and keep yourself semi-busy as you still draw from your retirement benefits. This will keep you engaged in your social life and contribute to perhaps a longer life, for work of many kinds keeps your wits about you!

But for many individuals, they have had their sights on retirement for a long time and know exactly how they wish to live out the remainder of their life. Most of these people contribute to causes they are passionate about that they have not had the time for throughout their younger years, whether it is helping with disaster relief, autism, food insecurity, etc. Or they venture into things that utilize the skills they have been performing for years to help others. Those with a "second career" tend to enjoy their retirement more than those that hated what they did for a living and see retirement as a time to do nothing end enjoy themselves. Those engaged in these types of second careers are more energized and feel much more fulfilled as they used the knowledge they acquired throughout their lives to bring new meaning to the lives of others and beyond.

Investing Before, During, And After Retirement

CHAPTER 5:

MONEY: YOU DON'T NEED $1,000,000.00

How to Create a Budget on Retirement Income

What are some of the factors that affect your budget while you are still working? Sometimes you do not know what income you will bring home. When you are in retirement, this doubt about how much you will have each month is gone. It makes it easier for you to budget your money for certain expenses.

So, if you need to go back and look at the list you used to help you determine if you will have enough in retirement, go through the steps outlining how to create a budget on retirement income.

Step 1: using a program online, spreadsheet, or piece of paper. Write down your monthly social security income. Since you may not be retired, use the projected amount of your last social security statement to make your calculation. You can also call to speak with a social security representative to determine inflation rates and get the amount you should expect in retirement based on working full time until your retirement date.

Step 2: do not include any pension, 401K, or savings that you have, when you write down your "retirement income."

Step 3: write down basic living expenses. The expenses in this list need to be things that you cannot live without paying. Yes, you could live without insurance, but the costs should something occur are too much—you could lose everything trying to recover from a house fire or health scare. So, insurance goes into basic expenses.

Also, note dining out and entertainment are not included (those are luxuries) not something you need for survival.

Step 4: take your social security benefits and minus your expenses. Do you have anything left or are you at a deficit? You may be at 0 or in a deficit depending on how much your monthly income is. Some people only get $700 per month, so it is not enough to cover their housing, let alone food and other essential needs.

Step 5: based on the calculation above, what do you need from your retirement savings to cover the basic living expenses? You will need to take that number and add a percentage to what you remove each month to your budget.

From this budget on your retirement income, you also know whether you should keep a part-time job to help you afford basic living expenses or some luxuries you want to have in your life, such as travel expenses.

Investment Channel

When it comes to choosing the right investment channel, it is sad that there is no method or formula that you can use in determining which is best for you. If you must invest, then you need to pay utmost attention to three things which are:

☞ Your investment has to be capital that is preserved.

☞ It has to be liquid.

☞ And a profitable investment.

However, there are lots of investors who have discovered that some profitable investment channels are completely focused on investing such as investing money into digital currency like bitcoin. In the time past, bitcoin turned out to be a bad investment as it failed to meet up the three criteria listed above, but it has since improved and become a common investment channel.

Furthermore, some investors only think of making a skyrocket return on their investment as soon as they make it without thinking of the possibility of risk being involved in the said investment. That is why most people keep searching for a highly profitable business investment where they can make double their investment as soon as possible, and in most cases, it becomes a flop. The truth about investment is that both the risk involved and the returns you get from the investment work hand in hand.

Therefore, while you are trying to select the best investment channel, you should endeavor to match your risk profile with that of the product you are about to invest in. Some investments are high risk with very high returns, while the low-risk investment comes with lower returns. Hence, choosing which is favorable to you is essential. On that note, we will be giving you a list of some investment channels that you can consider investing in; but before delving into it, you should have it in mind that investment products have been grouped into two categories, which are financial assets and non-financial assets.

Direct Equity

There are various types of stock out there, and picking the right one can be very challenging, but then again, not everyone is interested in investing in stock because it is one asset that is found in the volatile class without any assurance of returns. It is one thing to decide to invest in the stock; however, it is also another thing to time when to buy and when to exit because that part seems to be difficult. Investing in stock is more like "after the tunnel comes to light," because even though the stock market has a very high risk, dealing with equity delivers higher returns than any other stock.

Furthermore, due to the high risk involved, like you losing all your capital or a huge part of it, you can opt for the stop loss method to help in curtailing your loss. By using the stop loss method, you need to place an order to sell your stock in advance and at a certain price. Also, for you to reduce the risk involved to an extent, you don't need to depend on one stock, you should diversify and invest in other stock markets and sectors. Since you are thinking of investing in equity, you need to open a Demat account where you can buy and sell your shares. Equity is one investment channel that is high risk and gives a higher return.

Banks

To most investors, investing in a fixed deposit at the bank is one of the safest methods of investing, especially for people in India. When you place your money in a fixed deposit, you get interest in it quite often. It all depends on you, but you should know that the longer you leave your investment in a fixed deposit, the more interest you get.

Although investing in a bank is great and almost the safest investment, it is still nice to invest half of your savings there and think of another investment channel to invest the rest.

Digital Currency

Another great investment channel is digital currency, which has become a big hit for the past few years to date. There was a time when investing in bitcoin was a bad idea because of its slow or no return at all, and at some point, in the last few years, it failed completely. However, in recent times bitcoin has become very popular, and investing in it seems to be a great investment as it has grown really high. Just like the stock market that usually fluctuates, so does the bitcoin investment channel; it is not steady and is very risky since the currency doesn't have any value. However, don't be discouraged because the world has grown rapidly and everything has gone digital. This means even digital currency will become very valuable, and investing in it will fetch you high profit.

Furthermore, you need to know how to go about the business, know when to invest and when to pull out your investment because though the interest rate is very attractive and tempting when it falls, it might be difficult to recover from it.

Senior Citizens Saving Scheme

For most retirees looking for an investment channel, the first thing that comes to mind is investing in a senior citizen's saving scheme that is meant for either senior citizens of early retirees. The saving scheme can be accessed from either a bank or a post office, but it is only meant for people that are above 60 years of age. The senior citizen saving scheme has a five-year tenure, of which one can easily extend with another three years if you wish, and the extension can only happen once your scheme matures. There is an investment limit that might not be convenient for you, but you are allowed to get more than one account. The interest you get on your saving scheme can be paid quarterly and it is fully subjected to tax. Once you have invested, your interest rate remains the same until your scheme matures, but then the interest is subjected to be reviewed quarterly.

Real Estate

Real estate investment is one investment channel that is commonly talked about and more people are beginning to invest in it. Most people make the mistake of considering the house they live in as an investment, which is not supposed to be so because the house you bought to live in it for yourself. However, if you acquire another property, that can be your investment. Buying a property in a strategic location is one factor that determines how valuable your property is, and if you are purchasing the property so it can be put up for rent, then it should be in an environment that can earn you good rental value. When you invest in real estate, you can be sure that you will get returns in two amazing ways, your property value will appreciate with time and so will your rent value.

However, with all the sweetness and excitement that comes with investing in real estate, it still has its own risk. One risk is getting approval from the government to put up your property for rent and then the real estate can appreciate really fast, but a time will come when the value of your property will become lesser than the value you purchased it. Real estate is very exciting and no one ever truly notices when trouble comes to paradise, hence, as a real estate investor, you need to be very careful and watchful. Once the value of your property goes down, it becomes very difficult to come up again.

Gold

Investing in gold is an amazing investment channel as gold is very valuable with high investment returns. But purchasing gold is a thing of concern, especially if it is in the form of jewelry because you will be worried about keeping it safe and the high cost involved. It is one thing to purchase gold and another to make it, which is also almost as expensive as the purchasing power, especially if you have a special design in mind. However, you can also invest in buying gold coins from the bank or you can own paper gold, which happens to be more cost-effective. Investing in paper gold can be possible in a stock exchange market using gold as the asset underlying. Another option of gold investment is the sovereign gold bond and gold mutual funds. However, while investing in gold, you should note that the value of gold can be greatly affected by some unforeseen circumstances like a conflict, or interest rates might be increased by the Federal Reserve.

Pension System

A pension can be said to be a long-term retirement plan as it is an investment you begin to make when you are working. The national pension development scheme is a mixture of equity, fixed deposits, government funds, etc. Hence, if you are investing in the pension system you can choose your investment pattern, which also depends on the amount of risk you are willing to take.

Securities

One very profitable investment channel that grows well is the security investment, which is stock. Although, sometimes the stock market can fall greatly, but then it is a very lucrative investment. Over time, the stock market has grown greatly, but its sustainable growth is not stable, and sometimes it can be affected by market forces. Investing in security is a good one as it meets the criteria of a good investment that is liquidity and profit, especially if you are trading with a leading company that reserves investor's capital. The stock market is very large, hence, making available enough opportunities for everyone to invest in the market. There are various leading companies selling shares and attracting foreign investors, which makes the market very interesting and attractive. As interesting as the stock market might be, it has a high potential risk, because once the number of shares falls, it might go lower than what you bought, which causes a heavy loss. However, when the price of shares skyrocket, you tend to make a massive profit in returns for your investment. For this reason, investing in securities is a very good investment channel, so you need to look at the brighter side.

Get a good stockbroker to help you manage your shares and tell you when to buy shares and when to sell them to make a massive profit. Your stockbroker will always read financial reports of the stock market, understand how it is being managed and can evaluate the business, and let you know how good it is at the time. Most companies are working really hard to push the price of their shares higher so their investors can get enough profit from it.

Equity Mutual Funds

Equity mutual funds are more like investing in equity stocks. Investing in equity mutual stocks means you have to invest 65 percent of your assets in both equity and any instrument that is related to equity. To invest in this channel, you need to get a fund manager who can help you in trading your funds in a way that will generate many returns for you. Your equity scheme can be categorized according to the sectors in which the investment was made or according to market capitalization. Also, it can be categorized either as domestic or international stocks, so your fund manager can help you in categorizing your investment and know which will favor you.

Debt Mutual Funds

If you are an investor who needs steady returns, then the debt mutual funds investment channel is perfect for you. It is less volatile and can be considered as not too risky. The debt mutual funds are an investment of fixed interest that generates some securities like treasury bills, corporate bonds, commercial paper, and every other instrument that can be found in the money market. However, you should note that there are still risks in the debt mutual funds investment channel that you need to understudy before investing in it. If you are not used to the money market thing, you can employ a manager that is conversant with the money and stock market to help you in making your investments.

Public Provident Fund

This is one major investment channel people turn to because of its long-term tenure. You get to invest for as long as 15 years and your compounding interest becomes tax-free and increases by the year. The public provident fund happens to be a very safe investment because of its sovereign guarantee backing system. The best part is that the interest rate is always reviewed by the government quarterly, making it a more interesting investment channel.

When you have decided on the channel you will like to invest in, you need to understand the value of the investment channel and how legit it is. As an investor, you should also be aware of the fact that if you decide to go into the stock market and choose the leading companies that have come with a high and attractive price, can be too risky because when it falls the value becomes very low. So, if you are not involved in finance, get a stockbroker that knows the dos and don'ts of the market. If you also decide to go into the real estate sector, ensure that wherever you decide to get your property is a place that aligns with the rules and regulations of that city. Everything needs to be legal.

However, note that some of the investment channels listed above are either linked to the financial market or fixed income. Whichever it is, it is for wealth creation and they have the potential of giving you high returns as well as high risk.

Basically, any good investor should not shy away from a promising investment channel because of risk, rather go through the process and know if the risk is something that can be managed since every business one ventures into has its own risk. Also, it is important to have multiple investments so you can enjoy your retirement tenure, but while at it, keep the risk, time frame, and tax in mind.

How Much Money Will You Need to Retire?

The truth is that there is no single number that can assure everyone of a sufficient retirement. The amount will depend on a lot of factors like your target retirement age, your expenses (including medical expenses), and your preferred standard of living.

The good news is that you can establish a reasonable amount sufficient enough to cover your needs during retirement. If you plan in advance using conservative figures, you can definitely save a nest egg that is adequate to last you throughout your retirement years.

Steps You Can Take in Finding Out How Much Money You Need to Retire Comfortably

Compute for the Amount Equivalent to 65 percent to 70 percent of Your Current Yearly Living Expenses

Many expert financial planners recommend that this is the ideal place to begin computing how much you will require during retirement. It does not mean that you should end with this amount, though. Remember that your needs change, especially because of your extended life expectancy.

When you live longer, it means that you will need to take care of your health for a longer time, which will require additional expenses. If you wish to live a good and comfortable life during your retirement years, you will also have to allot extra money for entertainment, travel, and other activities that you can take pleasure in. The 65 percent to 70 percent estimate will be sufficient under the following conditions:

- ☞ You will have no housing expenses such as mortgage or rent.
- ☞ You will not have any expenses related to work such as eating out for lunch, business attire, and commuting.
- ☞ Your kids will be independent financially.
- ☞ You will have zero debts when you retire.

Calculate the Costs and Expenses That You Will Add or Subtract From Your Living Expenses During Retirement

To help in your calculation, you can answer these questions:

Do you wish to travel during retirement? If your family does not live near your residence, you may have to allocate funds for plane fare or gasoline for long drives to visit your family. Have you always wanted to visit other countries or even just travel around the United States? If your answer is yes, you need to start saving for your travels.

Is relocation an option for you? If your current area of residence is quite expensive, you can opt to sell your property so you can purchase a new house from a less expensive area. You can then place the difference in various investments that can help you in building your retirement funds. You just need to ensure that you consider how hard it is to lug firewood or shovel snow during wintertime.

Will you be able to continue working even after you have reached retirement age? Some people look forward to retirement age so that they can stop working for other people or they can enjoy a more flexible work schedule. Some professionals such as lawyers and CPAs continue working in their professions for several more years after reaching the retirement age.

Do you have any existing savings and investment funds that are allocated for your retirement? To determine how much additional retirement funds you need to save up for, you need to take into account any existing funds that you can rely on during retirements, such as the pension provided by your employer, royalty income, trust fund, or a 403b or 401k account that you have been contributing to.

Take Inflation Into Account

The dollar that you own now will not be able to buy the same amount of purchases 10 or 20 years from now. If your total yearly expenses are $65,000 and you estimate that you will need 70 percent when you retire (or $46,000), you need to realize that your $46,000 will not be enough to sustain your living expenses in 20 years. As such, you need to recalculate your estimated annual expenses by incorporating a conservative annual inflation rate of 3 percent. For example, $46,000 in the year 2015 is equivalent to $53,326 in 5 years or in 2019. This is computed as follows:

YEAR	AMOUNT	INFLATION RATE	AMOUNT
Year 1	46,000	x 1.03	47,380
Year 2	47,380	x 1.03	48,801
Year 3	48,801	x 1.03	50,265
Year 4	50,265	x 1.03	51,773
Year 5	51,773	x 1.03	53,326

Estimate the Number of Your Retirement Years

A lot of people do not really wish to think of their own mortality. If you want to properly plan for your retirement years, however, you do need to know the length of time you expect to be around after you have reached your retirement age. You can go online to look for a life expectancy calculator.

Make Plans for Your Heirs

This is purely optional. It is up to you if you want to leave something behind for your kids or if you wish to leave a portion of your estate to your favorite charitable institution. If you want to leave a legacy after you are gone, you need to incorporate it into the amount you want to save for your retirement funds. You also need to ensure that you have drawn up a will so that your estate and funds will be allocated as you want them to be.

Start Calculating Your Target Retirement Savings

Based on the previous steps that you have completed, you can use an online retirement calculator or a spreadsheet in computing how much you need to save every year starting now until your target retirement age.

CHAPTER 6:
THE STRATEGIES OF SUCCESS: LIVE THE
LIFE YOU DREAM OF

Before Retirement: Prepare for the Best

Thinking about retirement and leaving your business behind can be scary. For a lot of people, retirement is a time of life that can be described as emotionally difficult. There's the fear of leaving your business to the care of someone else and the possible emptiness of this new phase of life. However, it doesn't have to be all about that, and it certainly does not have to be painful for you. If prepared emotionally, retirement can become an exciting and wonderful stage in anybody's life. To have an understanding of the emotional stress that most people go through when they face retirement, as well as the tips in overcoming these fears, we will take a good look first at the challenges that often come with this period of life.

Emotions Involved With Retirement

People experience a wide range of emotions when they undergo retirement. First, there is a fear of the unknown. Although a lot of people today start saving money early on in their lives in preparation for their retirement, few actually think of what they are going to do once they get there. There are work-oriented people or people who have been raised with extremely strong work ethics who think of retirement as something like falling off a cliff. These people fear the lack of structure and organization in life after retirement, and not knowing what to do when they retire brings them fear.

Another emotion that is commonly felt by retirees is depression. This is especially true for people who have behaviors and emotions that are closely related to their careers, such as businessmen. They find it difficult to cultivate new interests, and they fail to seek help in doing this. When people fail to develop new hobbies or interests that are meaningful and could occupy a majority of their time in retirement, they may start doing things out of sheer boredom such as watching too much television, doing vices such as smoking, drinking or gambling, or slipping into depression. The trend of depression is increasing especially in the elderly. The lack of stimuli that comes from being occupied with something, e.g., work, can lead to boredom and ultimately to depression.

However, more positive emotions are also involved in retirement. There is a sense of freedom and relief. For a lot of people, how they spend their time has been controlled, structured, or dictated by their parents, instructors or teachers, their kids, and employers. Therefore, the fact that they have total control of their own time is something that they find relieving and wonderful. At their age when work is no longer a part of their life, they can pursue the dreams that they have been shelving for a long time or whatever else they want to do in their own time. Having their own clock and being flexible is something they anticipate and find exciting. Most may use this newfound freedom to do things that they have always wanted to do but lacked the time to such as home repairs, gardening, volunteering, traveling, or golfing every single day.

Tips That You Can Do to Emotionally Prepare for Your Retirement

Permit Yourself to Explore This New Stage of Life

Especially for goal-oriented people, trying out new things such as taking dance classes, writing a book, finding a piano instructor, or beginning a new career can be hard. They often fail to immerse themselves in one particular activity, and once they find that it is not their cup of tea, they will let themselves quit the lessons or classes without even completing it. The first thing for retirees to learn is to stretch their activities and their way of thinking, and to be more open to new possibilities and options.

Always Have a Plan B

Some people only want to do a specific activity for a long time, such as playing golf every day or keep a long list of things to do, and find that they are bored after one or two years. If you find yourself in this situation, it is helpful to think of other additional activities that you may want to do in the future if you find yourself doing the same thing over and over again for a couple of years, and then asking yourself "Now what?" Some retirees feel at ease in knowing that they have prepared well for their retirement.

Seek the Help of Others

There are life coaches, as well as retirement coaches who will be able to provide you with enough guidance and assistance in clarifying things that you may find confusing, including your role as a retiree. They can also help in making you understand what

106

things you want in life and how you can work to achieve these things. Having your own financial planner can also help in providing you with peace of mind, as well as an action plan for you to follow, even if you find that it is unnecessary for you. If you are going through serious emotional struggles and difficulties, then you may want to see a therapist such as a social worker, licensed counselor, or psychologist to help you get over the emotional aspects of retirement.

Look at Your Retirement as the Beginning of a New Adventure

In a lot of cases, retirees do not realize immediately that being in their 50s to their 70s is an entirely new place for them physically, emotionally, spiritually, and mentally. They are no longer the same as they were when they were in their 20s to 40s when the goals they were trying to attain were different. At this stage, there is often less desire in retirees to be competitive and try to prove something later in their lives. Also, they have less energy than in the earlier years. They are still healthy, talented, and active and may be at a point where they wish to give back to the causes that they believe in, and help the younger generation carve out challenging and fulfilling new roles.

Retirement: It's Not the End But a New Beginning

Preparing Your Own Business for Retirement: Four Retirement Options You Can Take

Being the owner of a small business is by no means an easy task. There are numerous struggles that owners have to face from the very beginning like finding the start-up capital, identifying the target market of your business, hiring workers and managing them, and finally figuring out ways and methods for you to grow and develop your own small business. However, one of the biggest hurdles that almost all business owners fail to think about, at least during the early business stages, is creating an effective retirement plan that will protect their future. If what you did before starting up your business was leaving a job that had retirement benefits, you will find it impossible to save for retirement without having mandatory pre-tax 401(k) contributions, as well as an employer that is willing to match this.

The biggest goal when it comes to planning for retirement for business owners both online and offline is to save money for the future. Therefore, it's a really smart choice to start spending more time discussing options with your small business accountant, or a financial planner if you have one, to identify what is the best way to begin saving. The second most important goal for retirement planning is regaining your control over your future in a general financial sense. As the owner of a business, you hold the ability to make much more choices when it comes to dealing with your retirement funds. Here are some saving options that you can check out, along with each one's advantages and disadvantages.

Savings Incentive Match Plan for Employees (SIMPLE) IRA

This is a suitable option for a lot of small or online businesses. If the number of employees that you have is below one hundred and you earn more than $5,000 in 2021, this is a plan that can work for you. You can simply use forms that are already provided by the IRS, making it easy for you to do it. You can use the form 5304-SIMPLE if you choose to give your employees the freedom to pick where they want to invest their SIMPLE IRA contributions, or you can also use the 5305-SIMPLE form if your plan is to choose which financial institution to use for everyone. When you got everything set up in your new plan, the next thing for you to do is to notify the employees about these changes so you can begin. This is good because it is affordable to set up and is equally cheap to maintain. It also allows higher contributions that can allow employees to give as much as $12,000 into their account. However, the negative side of this is that the contributions can go against your 401(k) contributions, and there are large penalties that can be applied for those who withdraw early, such as a ten to twenty-five percent penalty.

Simplified Employee Pension (SEP) IRA

This is as simple and as easy to work with as the SIMPLE IRA. However, you may find it hard to maintain this if you have more than two employees. Setting up the SEP IRA is as equally easy as the SIMPLE IRA. What you need to do is to fill out the 5305-SEP form and then let your employees know for you to get started. Setting it up is easy. No mandatory contributions exist in this system, and any contributions that you do make will be tax-deductible. In addition, the contributions will also have no effect on other accounts in the IRA, and the plan can be terminated at any time without incurring any heavy penalty. However, on the other side, the employers need to make a hundred percent of all contributions, and the percentages of these contributions must all be the same as well. The plan also does not allow any employee to be left out, which means that it can become expensive for you if you begin to grow your business.

Solo (Individual) 401(k)

For owners of small businesses or individuals who are self-employed, this can be a great way for you to increase your savings for your retirement. The great thing about this is that there are a lot more possibilities when it comes to the contribution, and they can be flexible for employees as well. There is no fixed amount of contribution required in the Solo 401(k), so you can give less if the times are tough and more if you happen to have had a pretty good year. However, this is more complicated than any other options for IRA, and you will need to find an administrator to help set up your own plan. It will also cost you money in maintaining and setting up because there are administrator fees involved.

Defined-Benefit Plan

This works just like pensions, but with big businesses, this is becoming less and less common. However, this can be a wonderful method for online or small business owners to use to save their money. One of the positives about this plan is that contributors can give as much money as they can. This plan works well for well-to-do business owners who always have money to put in the bank to save. It can also be combined with any of the other three options provided here, given that it is so much different in characteristic from other savings accounts. Any contributions made for this plan can also be written off simply as business expenses, thus minimizing the business and personal income. However, the costs of maintaining this is high, and it requires you to commit a fund at a specific level for you to meet your payout, which is limited when you set up the plan.

The New Retirement Landscape

The "boom" in baby boomer retirement is on the rise. This mass stampede towards retirement runs alongside a notoriously unstable time in America. The world we live in has become complicated and challenging to navigate. The retirement environment today includes low-interest rates, volatile stock markets around the world, unprecedented longevity, increasing budget deficits, and financial ambiguity. These realities are creating unnecessary stress and anxiety in many lives.

Planning for retirement is not going to be as easy as it was for your parents. I'm not sure if companies give out gold watches anymore. I do know that guaranteed pensions are far and few between. Today, much more preparation will be necessary for a successful outcome.

On a personal note, I have heard some deeply troubling stories about retirement plans gone wrong, as I'm sure you have. None of us want to end up being a financial burden on our families during our retirement years. Running out of money is a very real possibility for those who don't take the time to prepare for retirement.

Personal Responsibility and Your Retirement Portfolio

Personal Responsibility Defined

The willingness to accept the importance of societal standards for individual behavior and to make strenuous personal efforts to live by those standards. No one but you is to blame for your retirement planning, or lack thereof, so make it count!

Baby boomers are facing a crisis—the first generation to ever live through times like these. Whereas once you could trust Social Security and your company retirement plan to secure a long and happy retirement, this is no longer the case. We have entered into an era of personal responsibility.

Employer retirement benefits have become much less significant over the past few decades. Only 20 percent of workers from the private sector will have access to a pension that pays out for life. When 401(k)s came on the scene, they were supposed to supplement the company pension. Now, for many, the 401(k) is the pension plan and you are responsible for funding it, choosing the best investments, and making sure that the money lasts appropriately. As a result, many boomers are realizing that they are not prepared.

It's also been said that the Social Security system is fundamentally flawed. In fact, the Social Security (OASDI) Trustees Report states that "significant uncertainty" surrounds the "best estimates" of future circumstances. It's up to you to make your economic security in retirement a personal mission.

We have an industry bursting with "rock-star" financial brokers who place the financial futures of their clients in a "one size fits all" strategy. Maybe they lack competence or understanding, but this doesn't work. When the stock market has a drawdown of 50 percent and half your portfolio has evaporated, the answer I most often hear my clients getting from their brokers is "don't worry, it will come back, everyone lost money." That just isn't true. "Everyone" doesn't lose money. For me, that's an unacceptable answer. It's a put-off and in my opinion, it's callous. With knowledge and genuine concern, portfolios most certainly can be protected from large downside risk.

People quite often have no idea how or why their current portfolio was constructed and invested the way it is. I find that many have no real interest in investing their life savings in a highly volatile stock market, but on the advice of "reliable" brokers, a large portion of their savings is subjected to very high risk. Ask anyone who was invested in the stock market as recently as 2008 how that feels.

As you enter retirement, you should understand that ultimately you have to assume ownership of your retirement portfolio, investments, and the income streams you hope to achieve. You'll need a sustainable plan that has the potential to generate reliable income for the rest of your life. That's the best way to ensure your success.

That's not to say that you have to get an entire education in Financial and Retirement Income Planning. Of course not! It took me many years to gain this kind of financial and retirement knowledge.

What it does mean is that you should take some time to educate yourself enough so that you can understand the procedures involved in sustainable retirement income planning. Reading this book is one step. You may want to enlist the help of a qualified financial advisor who specializes in retirement distribution planning.

A significant aspect of a planner's experience lies in the asset accumulation phase. Accumulating money while you're working and building a plan of distribution in retirement are two very different disciplines. I'll get into that in greater detail later on.

The right person will help you gain a basic knowledge of the process and help you design a plan that can generate reliable income that you can presumably count on for the rest of your life.

The last thing you want to do is decide that you don't know enough, stick your head in the sand, and hand the whole process off to someone else with no understanding of how and why your portfolio is designed the way it is. Be proactive about the hows and the whys of your portfolio design. Ask questions.

You may have been working with someone for several years and feel that you know them quite well. You may be comfortable, and it's easier than starting a new relationship. I understand that but be sure that you understand that planner's knowledge base regarding distribution planning before you head off to the golf course. Otherwise, you risk being extremely disappointed when it's too late to do anything about it.

Moving From Accumulation to Distribution

One of the most important things that you have on your side when you begin saving money for retirement is time. When you are 30, 40, even 50 years away from retirement, you can afford to take more risk with the way you invest your money. You want to accumulate as much as you can so that you will be able to generate a paycheck when you're no longer employed.

When you're working and putting money aside consistently, you're performing a strategy called "Dollar Cost Averaging." Dollar-cost averaging actually works quite well while you are in the accumulation phase. Because you're adding money on a weekly or monthly basis, sometimes you're buying high and sometimes you're buying low—assuming you are invested in the stock market or some instrument related to it.

This averages things out for you and to some extent reduces your overall risk. It does not, of course, eliminate risk. Many fine and knowledgeable brokers can help you with this area. However, you will want to find someone who has your best interests at heart.

Hopefully, as you make your way closer to your retirement date, you've moved your portfolio toward less risk. You've spent the last

40 or even 50 years in the workforce. Maybe you've raised a family, owned a few houses, taken some great vacations, and along the way have managed to set aside a few dollars. Maybe you're lucky enough to have a company pension that you'll be able to count on, maybe not. And for now, lucky for us, Social Security is still here. Or perhaps you're already staring down at the "Golden Years." It came so fast that you've barely even had time to consider how to go about planning it out.

When you transition into retirement, you risk skyrockets in many ways. You are no longer working, and the weekly paycheck stops. All of the money that you have saved in your life is now finite. The decisions that you make will impact your quality of life, as well as your family's.

There is an essential shift that should take place concerning how you handle your assets when you transition into retirement. As you now know, the accumulation phase is concerned with building your retirement nest egg. The ultimate goal is to maximize your investment and savings returns over time. Then, when you reach your chosen retirement age, strategies must change.

As you move into the distribution phase, things get more complicated. You will need to monitor your withdrawal rate. This is extremely important. As an example, if you haven't moved to a safer haven and you are withdrawing 5 percent or $25,000 per year from a $500,000 portfolio, and that portfolio losses 30 percent, its value is now $350,000. If you make no adjustments to your withdrawal, that same $25,000 now represents 7.14 percent of your portfolio. That's a very big difference.

You'll want to take a closer look at taxes and strategies available to reduce them on an ongoing basis. Let's not forget about medical costs, inflation, and large ticket items to name a few. You'll also want to consider balancing your investments for a safer, more reliable portfolio. The ultimate goal of a sound retirement plan is to keep your nest egg intact, with enough money to cover seen and unforeseen events for the rest of your days while still maintaining the lifestyle you desire.

Investing Before, During, And After Retirement

CHAPTER 7:
WHAT DOES IT MEAN TO LIVE WELL AFTER RETIREMENT

How Does It Feel to Be Properly Retired?

Do you believe that retirement is your ticket to finally start pursuing those dreams and life passions? Many years ago, a lot of people believed in this notion. However, you should realize that there is no more reason to wait for retirement for you to be able to do all those things. Of course, upon retirement, you'll have a significant amount of money to spend. However, will this be all that you would need to do those things that you are dreaming about?

Take for example those adventure-filled travels that you want to embark on. If you will wait until you have reached 65 and older before you do this, you really can't do a lot. Will you still have the stamina to climb those steep trails in the mountains? Can your body take the pressure of extreme sports? Will you be able to keep up with your trip buddies when you go country hiking? These are just some of the best examples of why you shouldn't delay pursuing your dreams and passions anymore.

It is all about aiming to achieve that sense of fulfillment and happiness before you even retire. Nobody could guarantee that when you reach retirement age, your health will still be in its prime levels. A retired life should be focused on enjoying what you have accomplished and done during your younger years. This makes more sense most especially when you really envision the later part of your life as peaceful, contented, and not having any regrets about things.

120

Don't let your current job hold you back from doing what you really love. If you have been working with your company for a long time already, use your leave or vacation privileges. If this isn't possible, find organizations or groups of people who might be sharing the same passion and dreams as you are. Seek advice on how you could pursue your dreams at this point in your life. Learn about the success stories of people and pick lessons from them that you can apply to your situation.

When you are near retirement, there is a possibility that you have already made significant investments. If this is the case, use this as a motivation that you can really start pursuing those dreams and life passions without fear of losing your current job.

What Is the Best Place to Live?

If part of your retirement means starting somewhere fresh to enjoy your time of leisure and relaxation, the only challenge is finding somewhere that is a nice location that fits within the means of your budget and fixed income.

Bakersfield, California

Why not spend your golden years basking underneath a California sun? With all the perks of Cali and affordable living, you cannot beat this town! The average rainfall is 6.75 inches and there is a whopping 272 days of sunshine each year!

- ☞ Annual amount for groceries: $3220.
- ☞ Annual amount for rent: $7,000.
- ☞ Annual expenditures: $42,071.

St. Louis, Missouri

Many awesome services proudly serve senior citizens and retirees in the friendly St. Louis community. One of the best entities is the St. Louis County Age-Friendly Community Action Plan that provides volunteer drivers for those that need to get around when they can no longer drive on their own, calls to check in on senior health, home repair, legal assistance, and tax preparation are also included! There are also many historical sights to see and feast your eyes on!

- ☞ Annual amount for groceries: $3210.

- ☞ Annual amount for rent: $7225.

- ☞ Annual expenditures: $42,049.

Gainesville, Florida

Located in the middle of Florida, this town is the home of the University of Florida and Lake Alice, a natural reserve that you can spend a lot of time seeking out gaters, bats, and turtles, just to name a few species.

- ☞ Annual amount for groceries: $3,138.

- ☞ Annual amount for rent: $7,188.

- ☞ Annual expenditures: $41,996.

Columbia, South Carolina

In this region of South Carolina, many retired seniors are lining up to move here. With the amazing recreation and parks departments, there is a lot to offer regarding activities.

☞ Annual amount for groceries: $3,397.

☞ Annual amount for rent: $7,419.

☞ Annual expenditures: $41,885.

Phoenix, Arizona

If the beautiful weather filled with warm winters, hiking, and amazing golf courses is not enough to satisfy you, Arizona is also a state that does not tax Social Security income. Ensure that if deciding to move here you are ready to a feel of a bigger city and metro areas. Also, pack lots of sunscreens. Arizona enjoys more sunshine each year than parts of Hawaii.

☞ Annual amount for groceries: $3,058.

☞ Annual amount for rent: $7,523.

☞ Annual expenditures: $41,837.

Austin, Texas

Austin is one of the most rapidly expanding cities in the U.S. While it is made up of a series of suburbs, there is a nice small-town feel to Austin. You will definitely need a car in working order to ensure that you get to see all parts of this growing city.

☞ Annual amount for groceries: $3,085.

☞ Annual amount for rent: $9,085.

☞ Annual expenditures: $41,739.

Dallas, Texas

This city has a grand low cost for living expenses and its suburbs are sprinkled with a variety of stellar places for retirees of many ages to enjoy. Dallas has all the things big cities have, like pro sports, zoos, and lots of world-class dining opportunities.

- ☞ Annual amount for groceries: $2,963.

- ☞ Annual amount for rent: $8,417.

- ☞ Annual expenditures: $41,708.

Pensacola, Florida

At the far western end of the Florida panhandle lies Pensacola. If you want a nice taste of the beach for your time in retirement, this town is for you! Lots of sunshine and beaches to be enjoyed.

- ☞ Annual amount for groceries: $3,255.

- ☞ Annual amount for rent: $7,276.

- ☞ Annual expenditures: $41,541.

Sioux Falls, South Dakota

Healthcare in Sioux Falls is more than affordable and all the sights to see such as aquatic centers, miles, and miles of hiking and biking trails and parks are a big bonus.

- ☞ Annual amount for groceries: $3,319.

- ☞ Annual amount for rent: $7,151.

- ☞ Annual expenditures: $41,421.

Ann Arbor, Michigan

If you're looking for somewhere with a bit more of a youthful feel to retire to, this town is the perfect place for you! It is a college town full of young populations and has many great college sports team events.

- ☞ Annual amount for groceries: $2,973.
- ☞ Annual amount for rent: $8,321.
- ☞ Annual expenditures: $41,276.

Tulsa, Oklahoma

Tulsa is known as the city of lakes and has many beautiful gold courses to enjoy your afternoons at!

- ☞ Annual amount for groceries: $3,263.
- ☞ Annual amount for rent: $7,392.
- ☞ Annual expenditures: $41,055.

Salem, Oregon

Salem has been in the top 100 places to live in the world thanks to its natural amenities, cultural and recreational options, as well as affordable health care. Oregon is also another state that does not tax Social Security income.

- ☞ Annual amount for groceries: $3,111.
- ☞ Annual amount for rent: $7,310.
- ☞ Annual expenditures: $41,046.

Madison, Wisconsin

If you are planning to live solely off your Social Security of pension, you will be thrilled to hear that Wisconsin doesn't tax either of these incomes. There are five lakes, 260 parks, and more than 200 miles of path and trails to tread.

- ☞ Annual amount for groceries: $3,105.
- ☞ Annual amount for rent: $7,994.
- ☞ Annual expenditures: $41,041.

Kansas City, Missouri

There are many great transportation options to travel around this city, and in 2016 came up in the list of most affordable places to live at number 19.

- ☞ Annual amount for groceries: $3,045.
- ☞ Annual amount for rent: $7,366.
- ☞ Annual expenditures: $40,984.

Rochester, New York

If you want to retire somewhere that is not hot or cold all year round, Rochester has 4 distinctly beautiful seasons. The average temperature during the summertime is 78 degrees and in the winter it is 32 degrees.

- ☞ Annual amount for groceries: $3,067.
- ☞ Annual amount for rent: $7,421.
- ☞ Annual expenditures: $40, 586.

Salt Lake City, Utah

This city stands 4,330 feet above sea level and is home to many ski areas. This is somewhere where your family will for sure want to visit you during the holiday season!

- ☞ Annual amount for groceries: $3,066.

- ☞ Annual amount for rent: $7,619.

- ☞ Annual expenditures: $40,529.

What Do I Do Next?

You're officially retired and your opportunities are limitless! In truth, this realization could be a bit overwhelming, and the adjustments daunting. Never fear! I'm here to present some ideas to help you transition from a working stiff to a life of leisure.

You're perfectly entitled to spend a week or two lolling about and literally doing nothing if that makes you happy. After the dust settles and the excitement of celebrating your retirement wanes, it's a perfect opportunity to contemplate your situation and make some plans for the future.

The changes in a recently retired person's life will vary according to what they've been accustomed to doing. There will simply be more time to do the things they love! (And, if you aren't quite sure what you love, I'm going to help you find out.) If a person has always kept busy, the freedom to participate in their chosen activity will be a welcome respite. Golfers will enjoy more tee time. Shoppers will find exciting places to look for bargains. Hikers will seek out challenging trails. Pool loungers will have plenty of time to fine-tune their suntan.

An important step in paving the path toward a worry-free retirement is to take advantage of the freedom from obligations and get your house in order, both literally and figuratively. This is a perfect time to downsize. Clear away the clutter of unused possessions you've collected over a lifetime and you'll sweep the cobwebs of disorganization out of your life. This gives you the pleasure of starting fresh, with nothing holding you back from moving forward.

Set a date and begin sorting through your home, attic, garage, and storage areas. Depending on your hoarder status, this might take some time, but if you'll do a bit each day, it will soon be finished. You might be able to enlist help from your family and friends if you entice them by saying it's a party (things are much easier after a few bottles of beer and some pizza). On a more serious note, this process will make life much easier, not only for you but also for your family who will otherwise be forced to sort through your things after your death. Yea, you don't want that. Here are the four areas you need to consider when organizing your belongings.

Throw Away

At one time, you might have thought you could never throw away your child's kindergarten scribbles, but now they're disintegrated and it's time to dispose of them. Most people only need to keep tax records/receipts for three years, so throw away those boxes from the past forty years. You might need a shredder, or a big bonfire will work, especially if you're utilizing the party sham. Items that

128

are broken, melted, sticky, crumbling, rotted, greasy, mildewed, moth-eaten, mice nibbled, unrecognizable, and/or beyond repair need to go in this pile. No, you can't fix it, and it will make some lovely flames.

Give Away

These items are not trash, but things you don't need or want. They might have a bit of redeeming value, but not enough to try to sell. Clothes that don't fit (or you haven't worn in ten years) are welcome contributions to thrift stores. Old towels and blankets are treasured by animal rescue organizations. Get plastic bins for items you want to pass along to your children, grandchildren, or close friends. They might appreciate enjoying these things now rather than inheriting them after you pass on. Baby blankets (of now-grown children), nick-knacks, Christmas decorations, artwork, tools, jewelry, and mementos from family trips are just a few of the personal items you can pass on for others to enjoy. Sentimental items can be hard to part with, but knowing someone else will appreciate and value them will ease the pain.

Sell

Items of value can be sold through a variety of methods, and with a bit of time and effort, you'll accrue a nice fund for a vacation or other expenses. eBay is a popular choice for collectors' items and valuables. Designer clothes, handbags, and shoes can be taken to a consignment store for the best price. Furniture, vehicles, musical instruments, and large items are best advertised in a local newspaper or a "Thrifty Nickle" type magazine. Craigslist is widely used and often successful, but it has drawbacks, so be cautious when posting and communicating! Household gadgets, kitchen do-dads, trinkets, books, toys, and other small, inexpensive items sell quickly at yard sales and flea markets. Whatever does not sell, box it up and take it to a thrift store. Some charities offer free pick-up and you can schedule them to come at the end of your sale. Don't even think about saving it!

Keep

Trust me, there will be plenty left over after you've gone through the previous three steps. If you take time to organize the stuff you've kept, it will help your life run much smoother. Put photos in albums or sort them into small boxes by the year they were taken. Heirloom quilts, tablecloths, and other cloth items should be stored in an airtight container. Display your mementos and souvenirs in a curio cabinet so that you can enjoy them, rather than have them stored in a box under your bed. (Yea, I know about the under-the-bed boxes. Things go in there and might not be found until twenty years later.) Organize your garage or tool shed where you can quickly locate what you need when you need it.

You will be surprised how much lighter (physically and emotionally) you will feel when you've accomplished clearing away unwanted things and putting the rest of your possessions in order. Now, there's one other significant issue of the organization to address, and then you'll be free of my nagging and can move on to the fun stuff.

It's imperative that you review your important papers, make sure they are up to date and placed in a location that your next of kin or designated representative can find them. Here is a list of the vital information others might need. You may not need an attorney to create some of these documents, but you must refer to your state's requirements to make certain they are written, signed, and notarized in a legally binding manner.

Health Insurance Information

If you become ill or incapacitated, someone should be able to locate your health insurance information and speak to health providers about your treatment.

Living Will

In the event you are near death and unable to communicate, this document states your desires regarding extending extraordinary measures to keep you alive.

Power of Attorney

This is a written authorization giving your permission to allow another person to act on your behalf. You can make it as general or as specific as you want.

Will

This document provides your direction in appointing someone to manage your estate and/or the distribution of your property after your death. If you do not wish for your will to be read before your death, make certain you provide the name of the attorney or law office that will have the will on file.

Directive for Possessions Not Covered In A Will

Most attorneys won't want to detail everything you own, and who you want to have it after your death. You can type a list, have it signed, notarized, and added as an amendment to your will. It's also a good idea to discuss these wishes with your executor, or the person who will manage your estate.

Pets

Your pet will be confused and lost without you if you reach a point that you can no longer care for them for whatever reason. Arrange for a friend or family member to adopt your pet and provide a good home.

Funeral Arrangements

Many people have arranged their final wishes and, in some cases, have paid for their funeral expenses in advance. This might include your selection of a casket and burial plot or the process of cremation if that is your preference. Leave this information where it can be promptly located.

Life Insurance

Keep policies where your loved ones can find them and submit a claim. A recent report has shown that billions (yes, that's a B) of dollars of life insurance funds have been unclaimed because no one ever filed for them. They probably didn't even know there was a policy. If you have a life insurance policy, make sure your beneficiaries can collect the money you want them to have!

Many of these suggestions seem like common sense, but millions of people die without having a will or other directions to ease the burden of loved ones who are left to sort out the aftermath. Do you and your family a great favor by having these documents in order and easy to locate when needed?

CHAPTER 8:
A FRESH START, THE BEST

If this is what you really want, you'll know how much money will be needed to get it. In short, you'll be asking yourself the question of how much money you'd need to retire happy and contented. Retirement planning and consultancy experts are being tapped by many would-be-retirees today. However, you can figure things out even when they are not around.

Different financial experts will be seen and heard saying different things about how much money you should have saved up when you already have plans to retire. One expert says that if you are aged 65, you should have saved up at least 11 times your annual income. Another one is saying that your savings should be at least 33 times above your expected expenses for the first year of your retirement.

Now, even if the statements differ, common ground can be established. These experts are merely trying to say that a considerable amount of savings is needed before you can expect a comfortable retirement. Financial planning for retirement should be done at this stage. If you can still remember the retirement planning lesson you got in chapter 1, the planning that you will do here will be similar.

Some online calculators can help in your financial planning for retirement. Make sure that you can include factors such as life expectancy, inflation, future costs of medical services, nature of investments, and rate of savings. The use of these online calculators is commonly for free and comes with no obligations from the company that provides them. Through the computations that will be laid out, you will have a clearer idea if what you have is really enough for what you want when you retire.

Don't worry if you see that there are still issues to resolve. You still have time to prepare and a lot of your options can be found in the previous chapters of this book. Go through each section and see what course of action you can take to have enough for retirement.

So, now you have all the information that you need! Plan out your retirement as early as you can by using what you have learned from this book. Good luck and enjoy your life

Test-Drive Your Retirement

If you've taken the time to set up a financial plan to save for retirement and have considered how you would like to spend your time and the hurdles you may face once retired, you likely feel pretty confident about your plans. If, however, you are not sure you have everything figured out, carve out a chunk of time to take a sabbatical from your work and test-drive the experience of being retired.

Try It Out

If the timing of this transition remains in your control, you might consider one last step before making the big leap. Try it. Talk to your employer, and if that means talking to the person in the mirror, so much the better. See if you could take a mini leave of absence for a month or more.

If you will be retiring at the same time as a partner, try to structure a retirement tryout together. Your goal is to experience what it will be like being together 24/7. Use the time to discover how you envision your true retirement years together. Being able to do this without the distractions of work responsibilities is a gift. Use it well.

You will want to take enough time so it doesn't just feel like an extended vacation. To make the most of this period, try to form your days as you expect they might go. If going to the gym is to be part of your routine, commit to the number of hours you think you plan on committing and actually do it. Is volunteering in your game plan? Use the time to investigate where you want to give your time. Find out what each institution or nonprofit you are considering expects from its volunteers. Will spending more time with family and friends be a priority? Make dates to see them. Maybe you'll discover that their busy schedules prevent them from seeing you as much as you would like when you have no work distractions yourself. The overall goal of this trial period is to answer two questions:

☞ Are you ready (perhaps more than ready) to make the leap?

☞ Do you need more time before cutting the cord?

By giving yourself a window of time to try on the experience of stepping out of the full-time workplace, you can get a sense of what it would be like. Making this a defined "leave of absence" or just using up weeks and weeks of accrued vacation time, you will be reassured knowing you can return to the office and your steady paycheck.

138

Living Lean

One of the scariest aspects of discontinuing earning a paycheck can be the prospect of running out of money before you run out of years on earth. Even if you are planning on having a time where you combine receiving retirement benefits with part-time paid work, most likely you will eventually reach an age where you will rely solely on unearned income to cover your expenses. How will you know if you will have enough? One way is to make a conscious choice, even before your no work years, to cut back (way back) on your expenses.

The first step is to identify all the categories of expense. These would include:

- Housing: rent, condo fees, or mortgage.
- Taxes: real estate, state and local sales and income.
- Utilities: gas, electric, phones.
- Food and clothing.
- Entertainment.
- Travel.
- Hobbies.
- Health care.
- Automobile/transportation.

139

Charitable Support

If you look hard at each of these and consider where you can cut back, you can be well on the road to salvaging your retirement years by learning to live with less. How you spend your money is as much a habit as your morning routine. To change that routine, you will need to override a lifetime of patterned behavior. While it may seem like a daunting task, it can be done.

As part of your "trial retirement," you can begin to live a scaled-back lifestyle while you continue to earn a regular paycheck. Experimenting with ways to cut expenses while you are still working will help you sort out which bits of your overhead you can do without and which you cannot. Socking away the extra savings will fatten your "rainy day" cushion while helping you transition to a simpler lifestyle.

In much the same way your doctor may advise you that it is time to get the caffeine out of your diet, it may be time to reassess your spending habits. Getting rid of caffeine doesn't mean you can't drink coffee. It may just mean you need to develop a habit of drinking decaf. Cutting back expenses doesn't mean you have to eliminate something you need or enjoy. It may just mean having less of it or finding more economical sources. Whatever the area of your life requiring a change of habit, you will need to be deliberate about it.

Housing Transitions

Perhaps, one of the most visible signs of entering your third age will be a change of address. If you have been in a house for the decades in which you raised a family, it may no longer serve your needs. A recent television commercial for a real estate company shows an older couple looking longingly at their home, which they have just sold. The realtor leans into their car and reassures them, saying that they have sold the house but all the memories move with them.

Packing up memories may be a heavy emotional task, but the physical work involved in selling the family home can be backbreaking. Better to take this on in your early third age, before leaving work, for a few reasons:

- ☞ You will have more energy (both physical and mental) to deal with breaking down a home.
- ☞ Adult children may enjoy using furnishings and memorabilia they grew up within their own homes.
- ☞ You are liberating yourself from maintaining a property that had been needing more and more attention.

There may, in fact, be a magic window of timing for breaking down a household. If you wait too long into your retirement it almost becomes taboo to abandon the home in which you spent time with your family and in which your children were raised. Particularly if a spouse dies, the deceased spouse's extended family may view the home as a memorial to a time long past that should not be disturbed.

For many Americans, their home is a major piece of their net worth. It is yours to do with as you see fit. Deciding to shed it before you are fully launched into retirement may be a signal to your constellation of family and friends that you are writing your own script and do not plan to be an observer on the sidelines of everyone else's lives.

There is no doubt that retirement is still a key for you to achieve a significant amount of freedom to do what you want. However, there will be barriers or hindrances that are already present when this time of your life comes. Take this advice: don't wait until retirement for you to do those things that you really love. Act now and attain a good level of self-fulfillment!